INSIGHT POCKET GUIDE

SaBaH

Discovery
CHANNEL

APA PUBLICATIONS L
Part of the Langenscheidt Publishing Group

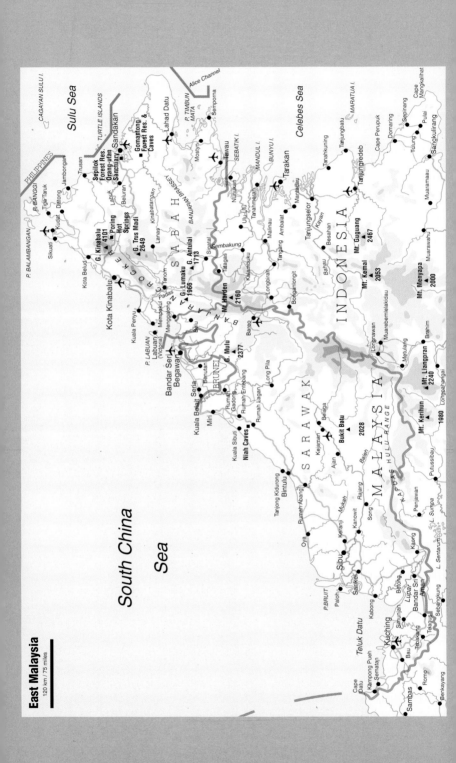

East Malaysia
120 km / 75 miles

Welcome!

This guidebook combines the interests and enthusiasms of two of the world's best-known information providers: Insight Guides, who have set the standard for visual travel guides since 1970, and Discovery Channel, the world's premier source of non-fiction television programming.

In the following pages, Insight Guide's correspondent in Sabah, Wendy Hutton, introduces you to time-honoured attractions and her favourite spots in this little-known but beautiful part of the world. Itineraries for day trips in and around the capital, Kota Kinabalu, are supplemented by longer excursions to the northwest and across the mountainous centre to the wildlife attractions, glorious white-sand beaches and superb dive sites of the east. Chapters on eating out, nightlife, shopping and sports, plus a practical information section covering travel essentials, complete this reader-friendly guide.

 Wendy Hutton, who's worked in Southeast Asia as a writer and editor since 1967, first arrived in Sabah in the late 1970s, drawn by the magnet of Mount Kinabalu. On her return a decade later, she discovered the many other facets of this corner of Borneo, and has since made it her base, delighting in its unique wildlife, virgin rainforests and incredibly welcoming people. 'I don't know any other place in Asia where the wildlife is so accessible, and where I am constantly delighted by so much variety, whether it's people, lifestyles, sports or terrain,' says Hutton, who loves nothing better than exploring remote corners of the state. She shares her love of Sabah and her discoveries in these carefully planned itineraries.

C O N T E N T S

Pages 8/9: the legendary Rafflesia in full bloom

HISTORY & CULTURE

Borneo has long nourished the world's dreams and fantasies. More than a millennium ago, Chinese emperors fastened their robes with buckles carved from the casque of the sacred hornbill and restored themselves with soup made from swallows' nests gathered in a land so strange that tales brought back to China were scarcely believed. For centuries, no one knew Borneo's shape or size, other than that it was a seemingly boundless island.

An Arab voyager, Ibn Batuta, sailing past North Borneo in the mid-14th century, gave the world its first description of Mount Kinabalu (and, incidentally, of the edge of a typhoon). Referring to 'the great Mountain of Clouds', he went on to say: 'at the foot of the mountain arise black clouds accompanied by winds which rise up the sea and wreck all that is found on that sea'.

Pigafetta, the Italian chronicler who accompanied Magellan's fleet on the first circumnavigation of the world, visited the Muslim Sultanate of Brunei in 1521. He spoke of the splendid carpets, silks, porcelain and brass canons adorning the Sultan's palace, but even more wondrous were the trees 'making leaves which, when they fall,

Murut tribesmen c. 1909 (courtesy Sabah State Museum)

are alive and walk'. Pigafetta's introduction to the brilliantly disguised leaf insects of the rainforest had him totally fooled.

By the 19th century, there were stories of head-hunting tribes; of impenetrable jungles filled with apes which resembled humans so much they were called 'man of the forest' (orang-utan), and of

Crocker range behind Kota Kinabalu

swashbuckling traders who could either become a white rajah or have their settlements burned to the ground by marauding pirates.

The world's third largest island was believed to be a vast, jungle-covered land where untold riches lay. Indeed, the old name for the island still used in the Indonesian portion, Kalimantan, means 'river of precious stones'; the name Borneo is in fact a Western corruption of Brunei. A huge lake was believed to exist on the south side of 'Mount Kinny Baloo', a lake 'so large that the land is not visible across it'. Maps drawn even as late as the beginning of the 20th century persisted in showing this non-existent lake, the subject of ancient legends.

Men were living in North Borneo more than 31,000 years ago; today's tribes, however, are believed to be descended from Mongoloid settlers who arrived in about 3000 BC. The land in which they lived was, since at least the 12th century AD, under the nominal control of the Sultan of Brunei. The north and northeastern portions of Borneo eventually came under the sway of the nearby Muslim Sultan of Sulu, in what is now the southern Philippines.

However, such matters as political control were supremely irrelevant to the scattered communities existing on fish and starch produced from the sago palm in the coastal regions, or hunting wild game and gathering the abundant fruits and other edible jungle plants in the almost inaccessible interior.

A traditional stilt village near Sabah State Mosque

Buying Borneo

Towards the end of the 19th century, during the height of the colonial expansion throughout Southeast Asia, Borneo inevitably attracted the attention of a number of Western powers: the Americans, Italians, Spanish, Austrians, British and Dutch, the latter two already established in the Malay peninsula and much of Indonesia. North Borneo eventually went to an Austrian, Baron Von Overbeck, who acquired rights from the sultans of Brunei and Sulu. In 1881, in partnership with Englishman Alfred Dent, Von Overbeck set up a company to administer the territory. Together, they obtained a Royal Charter and a year later, the British North Borneo Chartered Company came into being, with Von Overbeck bowing out of the picture.

From the very beginning, the Chartered Company ran the settlement of North Borneo as a business entity, bringing tremendous changes to both the land and its people. The company set about quelling piracy, planting tobacco, developing rubber estates and importing Indonesian and Chinese labourers to work in them. Bridle paths linking the various settlements were cleared, the telegraph was introduced, and work begun on the proposed Trans-Borneo Railway that was intended to link the east and west coasts. To finance all this, the Chartered Company demanded that taxes be paid by the natives.

This, however, so incensed the son of a Bajau chief, Mat Salleh, that he formed a rebel army and in 1897, totally destroyed the British settlement on Gaya, the island opposite today's Kota Kinabalu. He eventually retreated inland, building a fort in Tambunan where he was besieged and finally killed by the British in 1900.

Mat Salleh and his men weren't the only ones to resent the intrusion of the British. The isolated Muruts, who dwelt to the far southwest, felt their traditional lifestyle threatened and revolted against the British in 1915 in Rundum. This revolt was mercilessly quelled by the British, who somehow manhandled a cannon over impossible terrain to slaughter around 400 rebel Muruts.

The capital of North Borneo was established on the east coast in Sandakan (after its first couple of years in the northern settlement of Kudat). After the destruction of Gaya, the main west coast settlement was moved to the site chosen as the terminus for the Trans-Borneo Railway. This narrow strip of land, with the hills on one side and the sea on the other, was named Jesselton, after a director of the Chartered Company. Owing to the shortage of land, however, most native housing was perched on stilts over the sea; vestiges of these *kampung air* (water villages) remain even today, despite frequent reclamation pushing the water's edge further and further away.

In the first few decades of the Chartered Company's control, North Borneo produced adequate returns from its production of rubber, although its mineral wealth — in the form of copper, silver, gold and oil deposits — remained largely undiscovered. The jungle continued to provide the people with its traditional riches — rattan, wild honey and wax, *damar* (a resin), rare bezoar stones and rhinoceros horns (the latter two believed to have medicinal value).

Modern Times

North Borneo suffered badly during the Japanese Occupation of World War II and the Allied bombing that forced its surrender. The capital, Sandakan, was totally demolished, while in the town of Jesselton, just three buildings were left standing. In 1946, the capital was transferred to Jesselton, while North Borneo itself was handed to the British Crown. Unable to finance the enormous cost of reconstruction, the Chartered Company bowed out and North Borneo became a colony.

In 1963, after a series of discussions in which it was agreed that the two British colonies in Borneo (North Borneo and Sarawak) would retain a certain amount of autonomy, the Federation of Malaysia came into being. This linked the Malay peninsular states once known as Malaya with nearby Singapore (which quit the Federation two years later) and North Borneo and Sarawak, separated from mainland Malaysia by several hundred kilometres of sea.

North Borneo was renamed Sabah, the name which the locals had always called their country, but whose meaning no one seems able to agree upon. There was no mystery, however, about the new name for the capital when the colonial Jesselton gave way to Kota (meaning, City) Kinabalu.

Hand in Hand

An early visitor to North Borneo remarked that 'the diversity of peoples, the countless languages, dialects and sub-dialects used have all made the people more tolerant'. Sabah is Malaysia's most diverse state,

A 1949 colonial stamp

where the easy-going tolerance of the past still exists. At least 30 different ethnic groups make up Sabah's population of around 1.5 million, the largest being the Kadazandusun, who form around 30 percent of the population. The Kadazandusun are in reality a collection of many different groups with at least 10 distinct languages, although they are linked by similar cultural beliefs. Traditionally rice farmers, the Kadazandusun dwell on the coastal plains, the slopes of Mount Kinabalu and the rich coastal valleys in the interior. Although most of the Kadazandusun have converted to Christianity, some of the old primitive beliefs still hold sway, and in certain communities, priestesses still conduct age-old ceremonies to ensure a propitious harvest.

The coastal folk, long exposed to contact with the outside world, are mostly Muslim. On the east coast in particular, they lived in their boats (always ready for a spot of piracy) until encouraged on shore by the British North Borneo Company. Even today, many of the coastal fishermen remain poised between land and sea, living in houses perched on stilts at the water's edge.

Yayasan Sabah building, Kota Kinabalu

The biggest coastal group, the Bajau, originated several centuries ago in the southern tip of the Malay peninsula and migrated to the Sulu region, eventually migrating south to Sabah. The Bajau have adapted to the land with a vengeance since then, becoming renowned buffalo farmers and horsemen, particularly in the region of Kota Belud.

The Suluk and Illanun are also from southern Philippines, while the coastal Muslim Kadazandusun are known as Idahan, or Orang Sungei. In addition, there are also smaller groups of Visayans, Bruneians and Malays.

The most remote people are the tribes who were forced further and further inland by the more recent arrivals. These tribes — the Rungus living in the northwest, and the Murut, Lundayeh and Kelabit dwelling south towards the borders of Kalimantan and Sarawak — are the last of the traditionalists. Few of them, however, still hunt with blowpipes, and communal dwelling in longhouses is slowly dying out. Most of the Muruts and Rungus have exchanged animism for Christianity and, with the younger generation exposed to education and modern lifestyles, the traditional ways of life are inevitably eroded.

If you are fortunate enough to see a group of Sabahans in traditional dress at a festive occasion, the rich diversity of Sabah's culture will be immediately apparent: Murut men aquiver with pheasant feathers and clad in beaten bark cloth; Suluk girls looking like Oriental princesses in glittering golden headdresses and shimmering silk; Kadazandusun in gold-rimmed black fabric and wrapped with belts of silver coins; Rungus women jingle with tiny bells, draped with antique beads and intricately woven cloth, and Bajau men in gaily beaded and embroidered jackets and trousers, their folded headdress set at a rakish angle.

The Latest Wave

The cultural potpourri of North Borneo was further enriched by the Chinese, brought in by the British in the early 1880s. The first arrivals were the Cantonese from Hong Kong, mostly shopkeepers who found no demand for their skills in the new settlement. The next batch were hard-working Hakka farmers, all Christians from southern China, who proved to be such successful immigrants that the trend continued, making the Hakkas the biggest single Chinese group found today in Sabah. Quite uniquely for Southeast Asia, roughly half of Sabah's Chinese population are rural workers, as opposed to traders and shopkeepers in the towns. Today, the Chinese community forms the second biggest ethnic group in Sabah. Over the years, many Chinese have intermarried with locals, particularly the Kadazandusun, further adding to the almost bewildering ethnic mix.

Indonesian labourers from nearby Sulawesi, Flores and Timor, flocked to Sabah to join the workforce several decades ago, joined more recently by other Indonesians who labour in the oil palm, cocoa and rubber estates. Ethnic Filipinos fleeing the conflict between the predominantly Muslim Mindanao and the Philippine government arrived en masse during the 1970s when they were given safe haven by the state government. They have since been joined by thousands of illegal economic migrants who, while providing much-needed labour, present social problems yet to be solved.

Many Paths to God

Most visitors are surprised to learn that, unlike Peninsular Malaysia, Sabah is not a predominantly Muslim state, although Islam is the official religion, as in the rest of the Federation.

The majority of Sabahans are Christians, with Muslims forming the second biggest group. An astounding variety of religious buildings such as mosques, churches, Buddhist, Taoist, Sikh and Hindu temples and Bah'ai meeting halls all exist to meet the religious needs of Sabah's diverse people.

Economy

The first recorded export of timber from British North Borneo was in 1885, when a slump in world prices prompted a sugar plantation owner near Sandakan almost literally to cut his losses by felling his trees. It wasn't until almost a century later, in the 1970s, that Sabah's rich rainforest was fully exploited, and for the past couple of decades, timber has provided the state government's major source of revenue.

In dollar terms, Sabah's most valuable export in recent years has been crude petroleum, which is mined offshore. But because Sabah is allowed to keep only five percent of the revenue earned from petroleum exports, this potentially valuable contribution to the state's coffers is less important that its other major exports, palm oil and cocoa.

To slow down the rate of logging and to expand local manufacturing, there has been a shift away from exporting whole logs towards processed timber, such as sawn wood, plywood and furniture. Such a move requires sawmills, factories and the availability of skilled labour, all of which are in short supply in Sabah. Meantime, the state government is searching for ways to continue the felling of trees on a ecologically sustainable basis, so that the rainforest, of immeasurable value both to Sabah and the whole world, will not be wiped out forever.

As experts look to reforestation: planting of fast-growing softwoods, and using the forest for traditional resources such as rattan and medicines; others see an increasing interest in ecotourism as the answer to preserving Sabah's forests. Whatever the future may bring, today's visitor to Sabah still has the rare opportunity of being able to enjoy the amazing beauty and diversity of the rainforest in a world where this precious and fragile environment is quickly disappearing.

Tourism, while still not yet a major revenue producer, is increasing in importance in Sabah, as, indeed, in Malaysia as a whole. While there are a few foreign-owned tourism ventures in the state, the majority are both owned and run by local Sabahans, and provide abundant employment opportunities in a number of key locations. The recent proliferation of resorts and hotels along the west coast around Kota Kinabalu and the Kinabatangan River, as well as Sipadan and nearby islands, is a positive testament to the growth of tourism in the state.

Colonial-era bank note

Historical Highlights

AD 700–1400: Chinese annals record early trade between the Celestial Empire and the coastal settlements of north Borneo, including the Sultanate of Brunei.

1521: Magellan's fleet visited Brunei, an event which is recorded as the first contact between Westerners and the people of Borneo.

1577: The Spanish colonised the Philippines and brought the Sultanate of Sulu under their nominal control.

1662–74: As a result of wars of succession in Brunei, the Sultan of Sulu was promised the area that is now Sabah by Muhuideen, who failed to honour his promise on becoming Sultan.

1761: The British East India Company entered into an agreement with the Sultan of Sulu and founded a trading post on the island of Balembangan, near Kudat. The settlement was burnt to the ground by pirates in 1775.

1764: The Sultan of Sulu ceded all of North Borneo, including Labuan, Banggi and Balembangan islands, to the British East India Company.

1846: The Sultan of Brunei ceded Labuan island off the west coast of Sabah to the British Crown.

1865: The American Trading Company established the settlement of Ellena in Kimanis (southwest Sabah), after obtaining a 10-year lease from the Sultan of Brunei. The settlement failed after a year.

1875: The lease to Kimanis was sold to Baron Von Overbeck, who renewed it for another 10 years.

1877: Overbeck joined forces with the Dent brothers of London and signed new leases with the Sultan of Brunei for a larger territory, as well as leasing land from the Sultan of Sulu.

1881: Dent signed all his rights to North Borneo to a company that was granted a royal charter. Kudat became the first capital of British North Borneo, while trading posts were established on Gaya Island and Sandakan.

1882: The British North Borneo Chartered Company was officially formed, and in the following three years bought more land in North Borneo.

1884: Sandakan, which had first been settled at Kampung German in 1878 and was resettled a year later as Elopura, became the capital of British North Borneo.

1894–1900: Mat Salleh, a Bajau chief, constantly rebelled against the British presence, razing Gaya in 1897, until he was killed in a siege.

1896: Work was begun on the proposed Trans-Borneo railroad.

1899: Jesselton was founded on the mainland opposite Gaya and flourished as the railroad took shape.

1942: Japanese forces occupied Sabah.

1946: The capital was moved from Sandakan to Jesselton owing to the total destruction of Sandakan during Allied bombing raids at the end of the war. Sabah became a British Crown Colony as the Chartered Company could not afford to rebuild the war-devastated country.

1963: North Borneo became independent and reverted to its precolonial name, Sabah, on becoming a state of the Federation of Malaysia.

1967: Jesselton, originally named after a director of the North Borneo Company, was renamed Kota Kinabalu.

1985: Sabah became the first state in Malaysia to elect a non-Muslim State Government, run by the Kadazandusun Christian-dominated Parti Bersatu Sabah (PBS).

1994: Although the PBS won the state elections, desertions by PBS members resulted in the federal ruling party, Barisan Nasional (BN) taking over power. BN has won subsequent elections and continues to govern Sabah.

2000: On 2 February, Kota Kinabalu achieved city status.

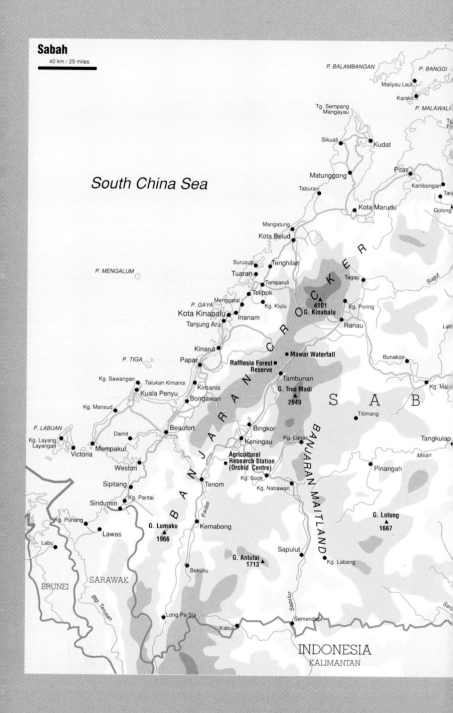

Day Itineraries

The itineraries in this section of the book range from a few hours to a full day. From your base in the capital, Kota Kinabalu, you can explore the town, its nearby islands and fishing villages, discover the rich beauty of Sabah's rare plant life and go horse-riding or white-water rafting.

The itineraries in the *Excursions* section that follows go further afield and require between two days and a week. Some of the tours, like Poring Hot Springs and climbing Mount Kinabalu start out from Kota Kinabalu, while others, like diving in Pulau Sipadan and exploring the fascinating Turtle Islands Marine Park require travel – by land or air – to Sandakan on Sabah's east coast.

Other more remote but no less exciting destinations like the brooding Danum Valley and the wetlands of the Kinabatangan River or the Caves of Gomantong, require at least overnight stays. For these destinations you must travel by air and road or, more commonly, on a package tour from Kota Kinabalu.

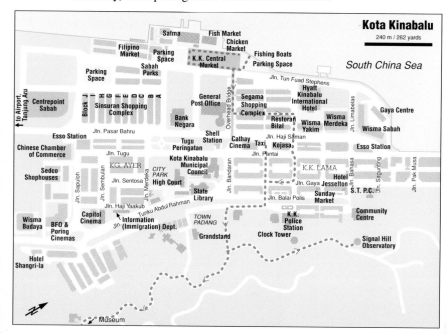

Kota Kinabalu

A jumble of produce at the Kota Kinabalu market

1. Kota Kinabalu Highlights

Feel the pulse of Kota Kinabalu with an early morning prowl through the Central Market, followed by a pause for breakfast. After the panoramic view from Signal Hill, the Sabah State Museum (closed on Friday) introduces the rich diversity of the state. View the impressive State Mosque en route to lunch.

Start this half-day trip before breakfast at 8am. Make your way to the north end of the **Central Market** (open daily dawn–5pm) and walk past the car park to the waterfront for a view of the brightly painted fishing boats. Across the channel and perched over the sea are the stilt villages of **Pulau Gaya**, home to several thousand Filipinos.

Enter the market at the back door facing the car park; this will bring you to a couple of stalls selling soya bean milk and delicious warm soya bean curd *(tau foo fa)*. For RM80 cents, the vendor will scoop the silkened curd from a huge stainless steel drum into a bowl and top it with sugar syrup. Sit on a nearby bench and enjoy.

Hunger satisfied, you can now wander through this huge Asian market, where you'll find everything from fresh fern tips to imported grapes, orchid plants to porcelain tea cups. Take your time and you will see colourful basketware, strings of what looks like huge white beads (dried yeast for making rice wine), and inhale the aromas of countless fresh herbs, roots and spices, local tobacco, areca nuts and betel leaves, and freshly ground local coffee.

The amazing array of food will have worked up your appetite. Climb the stairs at the north end of the market near where you came in and take the pedestrian bridge; later in the day, this is an excellent place to spot colourful characters selling traditional

Instant grated coconut

A Jalan Gaya shopfront

medicines, Rungus beadwork, wild honey and the like. Take the third exit to the left from the bridge and walk down into the **Segama Shopping Complex**. Pass the old Chinese men chatting at the base of the steps and continue down until you see **Restoran Bilal**, on your right.

Order a couple of *roti canai* and watch the performance of the Indian cook as he swings out a ball of dough in ever-increasing circles to create a light and flaky pancake. Tear off little pieces and dip them into the accompanying curry. Scrumptious.

Continue down the pedestrian mall, where the old-style stores are giving way to modern shops and fast food joints, and turn right into Jalan Datuk Salleh Sulong. Continue across busy Jalan Haji Saman, across Jalan Pantai (once the waterfront) and turn right at the quaint old Chinese liquor-cum-fabric store into **Jalan Gaya**. The heart of old Kota Kinabalu, this street – once full of traditional stores – is slowly changing as pedestrian malls and sidewalk cafes are being introduced, and traffic flow is restricted. The dining area outside Jesselton Hotel is particularly pleasant in the evening.

The row of shophouses on the opposite side of Jalan Gaya were the first to be constructed after World War II devastated the city. Look up on the hillock nearby and you'll see one of the three structures to escape bomb damage, the quaint **Atkinson Clock Tower**, built in 1905 in memory of the town's first district officer, who died of 'Borneo fever' at the age of 28. As recently as in 1956, the lights of the clock tower aided ships in their navigation; today, the tower is completely obscured by the surrounding buildings.

Turn right from Jalan Gaya and take a taxi from the nearby taxi stand. Ask the driver to take you up to Signal Hill to the observation point, then on via Jalan Istana to the Sabah State Museum – not the quickest but certainly the most picturesque route. The taxi will pass the **Padang**, an open green where the colonial British first played cricket in 1901, then turn left up to **Signal Hill** (along Jalan Bukit Bendera). Pause outside the **Signal Hill Observatory**; this was closed in 2000 due to landslides nearby, but you can still enjoy the view over the town and across the bay, where coral reefs play artist with the sea, painting it in jade, azure and turquoise, to Gaya island and down south to the luxurious resort at Tanjung Aru.

Jalan Istana cuts through a tunnel of greenery along the ridge of Signal Hill, passing old bungalows tucked almost out of sight

Sabah State Museum

and the **Istana** (palace), residence of the head of state. Shortly after, you'll approach the **Sabah State Museum** (open daily 9am–5pm, except Friday). Don't enter the main building, but turn right across the car park to the display of life-sized traditional houses, arguably the

Imposing Sabah State Mosque

most interesting section of the entire museum. Here you can wander about the longhouses and other homes of Sabah's major tribes, peep into the kitchens filled with typical cooking implements, the various tools and fishing traps used by the tribes, and see herbs, vegetables and medicinal plants in the gardens outside.

It's time now for the main body of the museum. The ground floor has an interesting ethnography section on the left, particularly the costumes, while to the right, the historical photos of Kota Kinabalu are worth a closer look. At the back on this side is a reproduction of a cave, complete with swallows' nests and the paraphernalia used to gather this precious commodity. The natural history display on the right side of the first floor is a good introduction to Sabah's flora and fauna.

As you come out of the museum, take the steep path down through the magnificent palm trees to the main road. You'll see the **State Mosque** just ahead of you. Walk closer and have a look at the beautifully propor-tioned domes and minaret, the golden Arabic characters swooping like birds over the soft grey stone. The interior of the mosque is somewhat disappointing, so skip it and consider having lunch instead.

Take a bus in front of the mosque and travel a couple of stops, getting off in front of the Anglican church just beyond the Karamunsing traffic junction. Cross the road to **Kompleks Karamunsing** and look for the ground-floor MAS office. To the left of this, just beyond the KFC out-let, is the **Bistretto**, where you can enjoy good salads and pasta, as well as pancakes and ice creams. Alternatively, go down the stairs near MAS; turn left and head to the back for Karamunsing Court, where around 20 food stalls offer a wide selection of Malay, Chinese and Indian food in air-conditioned comfort.

Atkinson Clock Tower

23

Swim in the crystal clear waters of this marine reserve, exploring the wonders of the coral reef; laze on a talcum-powder beach as hornbills fly overhead; and wander through a nature trail on one of the park's five islands – all this just minutes from downtown Kota Kinabalu.

If you prefer to have a beach virtually to yourself, and eat a picnic lunch under the shade of a tree instead of battling it out with crowds in a restaurant, do the following half-day trip on your own instead of booking a package tour.

The picturesque **Tunku Abdul Rahman National Park**, which was gazetted as a marine reserve in 1924, is made up of the following five islands: Gaya, Sapi, Mamutik, Manukan and Sulog. Of these, **Pulau Manukan** is the most frequented island, with facilities such as a restaurant, swimming pool, chalets where you can stay overnight, and masks and snorkels for hire (although it must be admitted there's little marine life to see off this island). All you need to do is find transport and go.

If you prefer somewhere more private, get your hotel to pack a picnic lunch or go to Tong Hing Supermarket in Jalan Gaya (open daily at 9am) to buy fruit, cheese, cold cuts, savoury buns or sandwiches, and drinks. Ask the butchery section for a chunk of ice to keep your food cool.

Police Beach at Pulau Gaya

Walk back to the waterfront in front of the Hyatt Kinabalu Hotel, near the Labuan ferry terminal, and bargain for a boat to take you to the island of your choice. Don't worry about finding the boats; hustlers will fall upon you the minute you near the waterfront, but take your time and be sure to choose a boat equipped with life jackets. Trips to the popular Manukan, Sapi and Mamutik islands cost around RM10 per person return; pay only when your boatman fetches you for the return trip. An alternative is to use the regular ferry service operated by KOKTAS, which leaves from Sabah Parks' jetty in front of the Hyatt for Manukan every hour from 8am to 4pm daily. The fare is RM10 per person for a return trip.

Underwater coral garden

Since Manukan gets crowded with locals on Sundays, you may want to head for **Police Beach**, located on the northern side of **Pulau Gaya**. The beach is idyllic except during the monsoon season from December to February. As the island is further away, it costs RM80–100 for a boat. The wonderful sweep of Police Beach is backed by forested hills. There is a trail leading across to the Park Headquarters on the other side of the island, with a boardwalk across a mangrove swamp just before you arrive. You could ask your boatman to meet you here after your one-hour walk across, or you could just luxuriate in the beauty of Police Beach for a few hours.

Another favourite spot is **Pulau Sapi**, a tiny island joined at low tide by a sand bar to Pulau Gaya, the biggest island in the marine park. Although the best coral in all the islands is found at Pulau Sulug (where a dive company now operates), there's some nice coral at the southeast tip of Sapi. If you snorkel out over Sapi's reef, you'll see brilliant fish in a kaleidoscope of colours: turquoise, blue and pink parrot fish, neon blue guppies, cheekily striped clown fish and lemon-yellow angel fish. Back on land, you're almost certain to see macaque monkeys in the trees near the shaded grassy picnic area, and you may well hear black and white pied hornbills.

Tour operators bring groups to Sapi for lunch-time barbecues and it can get very busy during peak seasons, so if you'd like some privacy, ask your boatman to take you to **Pulau Mamutik**. There's not much here apart from delicious peace and quiet, two lovely small beaches, a nature trail, a picnic area, toilet facilities and a scuba diving operator. As with all the islands, the beach drops off rapidly and you'll notice a dramatic change in the colour of the waters as you reach the edge of the reef.

On your return, walk along Tanjung Aru beach to the stalls and enjoy a refreshing young coconut drink as you watch the sunset. If you're hungry, try the delicious seafood at the open air Beach Seafood Restaurant nearby. Spicy banana leaf-wrapped stingray is a fine way to end a perfect day.

A fiery sunset at Tanjung Aru

3. Kinarut Trail Ride and Filipino Market

If you've ever sat on a horse, this is all the skill you'll need to go on a 2-hour trail ride through lovely rural scenery complete with lush padi fields, split bamboo houses, birds and butterflies. Cool off with a drink on a beach-front verandah then head back to town for a little souvenir hunting at the Filipino Market.

Call the **Kindawan Riding Centre** (tel: 088-225525) a day in advance and ask to be picked up from your hotel around 6.30am for the 20-minute drive down to **Kinarut**. The scenery near the beachside stables doesn't prepare you for the remarkably pretty rural valleys and gentle hills you'll be exploring this morning.

Comfortably astride your pony, you pass through Kinarut village, a quaint cluster of big old wooden shophouses. The road narrows and soon you're on a country lane, shaded by giant stands of bamboo and fruit trees. Dozens of birds provide a melodious accompaniment to your ride. Watch for butterflies, too, especially as you follow the stream.

Split bamboo houses float in a sea of emerald paddy fields which lap at the feet of the hills. If you're lucky, you may see groups of children shrieking '*Kuda, kuda!*' (horse), and sarong-clad women wading the water-logged fields with a fishing net. It's difficult to think of a nicer way to see, hear, smell and feel the countryside than at a gentle trot on horseback.

After your return to the stables, ask to be taken to the **Seaside Traveller's Inn** just down the road. Sit on the breezy upstairs verandah, order a tall tropical drink and enjoy the panoramic views of the beach and islands.

When you get back to your hotel, you'll probably want to take a quick shower and change before visiting the **Filipino Market**, on Jalan Tun Fuad Stephens opposite Sabah Parks' office. The market

Paddy fields near Kinarut village

Tempting goodies at the Filipino Market

is a huddle of wooden stalls separated by a maze of narrow alleys. Although many of the stalls seem to be selling the same curtains of shells, cascading macrame hangings, woven baskets, wood carvings and sunhats, look a little closer and you may find some original and unusual items. Be sure to bargain hard; you may get as much as one-third off the original asking price. Apart from Filipino handicrafts, there are several stalls selling Indonesian batik fabric, Iban baskets from Sarawak, and local Sabahan pottery (mostly the glazed, incised variety). There are piles of glittering stones, but don't expect to find real gemstones here; if you want these, or gold jewellery, shop at one of the real jewellery shops in Wisma Merdeka, Centrepoint or in the Segama shopping area not far from the Hyatt hotel.

Walk up past the main market and take the pedestrian bridge that leads to the General Post Office. By now, the bridge should be filling up with hawkers offering bottles of delicious wild honey, folk medicines, cheap trinkets and toiletries. Visually impaired musicians hang out here, and you can often spot a group of Rungus tribespeople. The most traditional women wear brass bangles and antique beads as they sit barefoot in black home-spun sarongs, stringing cheap bright beads into necklaces and bracelets. Their menfolk, often wearing a folded headcloth or *dastar*, squat over piles of locally produced tobacco, often sampling their wares while awaiting customers.

Go to the far end of the bridge, turn left down the stairs, and you're back in the main street of town. You might like to walk up the road a couple of hundred metres to **Wisma Merdeka**, where there are several shops specialising in Sabahan crafts *(see Shopping, page 62)*, as well as a couple of good bookshops. Alternatively, go to **Centrepoint** after leaving the Filipino Market and explore the many souvenir shops in this complex. By this time, you'll be ready to head back for your hotel or to go to lunch.

Two contrasting communities – the Bajaus in a traditional fishing village of thatched houses perched above the water, and the rice-growing Kadazandusun living in an idyllic valley – are both within easy reach of Kota Kinabalu. Visit a pottery factory en route, and end the day with a picnic and a swim in the river.

It is with some ambivalence that I recommend the following itinerary to the traditional villages of the Bajau and Kadazandusun peoples. The villages are off the beaten tourist track and the people are not used to being invaded by bus-loads of inquisitive visitors. To avoid being intrusive, please observe the basic rules of etiquette when visiting someone's home: do not walk into homes without an invitation, and ask before photographing women and older people (the children, on the other hand, will plead to be photographed).

You'll need to hire a car for this full-day trip. Pack a picnic lunch and swimming gear, and set off around 8am to avoid the hottest part of the day while you're exploring the fishing village. Take Jalan Tuaran out of town, turning left just beyond the huge Pu Toh Sze temple complex with its giant statue of the Goddess of Mercy in the grounds, into Jalan Tuaran Bypass. Follow this road, going straight at the roundabout 30km (20 miles) north of town and follow the signs towards Kota Belud.

Suddenly, the semi-industrial sprawl of Kota Kinablau's outskirts is replaced by rural scenery as picturesque as you'll find anywhere, with paddy fields, water buffalo, simple wooden cottages and a tangle of fruit trees, palms and lush flowering shrubs. All this will be framed against – if the weather permits – the dramatic background of Mount Kinabalu.

Bajau and Dusun Villages

25 km / 15 miles

South China Sea

The unusual ethnic mix – indigenous Lotud (a Kadazandusun subgroup), Bajau and Chinese – makes Tuaran an interesting little town, and its Sunday market or *tamu* is worth visiting.

Just under 5 km (3 miles) on the Kota Belud highway from the Tuaran town, turn off and turn left at the sign 'Kg Surusup'. Park your car and ask at the little store on the right for Haji

Standard transport at Kampung Penambawan

Abdul Saman, who will be happy to take visitors upriver by boat to the Bajau fishing village, **Kampung Penambawan**, for around RM20. If you are prepared to pay RM40–60 for an hour, he'll also take you to the river mouth *(kuala)*, an extremely pretty spot where the river and sea merge with sandbars, pristine beaches and shady casuarina trees – either swim in the surf or bathe in the river.

As you turn a bend about 10 minutes upriver from Surusup, Kampung Penambawan floats into view, an Asian Venice of sorts where dozens of *attap* (palm-thatch) houses linked by walkways cluster at the edge of the wide river. It is difficult to understand why this particular fishing village – less than an hour by road and boat from Kota Kinabalu – should have escaped the less attractive aspects of 'civilisation'.

Drying fish on the boardwalk

You won't see any TV aerials on the houses, plastic junk floating in the water and there are only a few corrugated iron roofs. As you explore, watch out for the pottery jars used for storing fresh water, women weaving mats from pandanus leaf, split fish or bananas drying in the sun, and villagers paddling along in dugout canoes from house to house. You won't miss the dozens of cats who do very well on a diet of fresh fish. The river provides a bounty of fish, as well as crabs and prawns, which are a ready source of income for the fisher-

Typical suspension bridge

men of Kampung Penambawan.

The Bajaus, believed to have originated in the southern tip of the Malay peninsula, came to Sabah via the Philippines. It might occur to you as you teeter for balance on some of the more precarious *nibong* palm walkways, that it's a good thing that the Bajaus are Muslim and therefore forbidden to drink alcohol; negotiating the walkways in a less than sober condition could be a challenge.

Leave the Bajaus behind and retrace your steps to Tuaran. When you come to the highway at the roundabout, take the A1 towards Tamparuli, Tawau and Sandakan. Further on, a blue signboard on the left indicates a right turn to **Tamparuli**. Turn right and continue for a couple of minutes until you pass the substantial white hilltop headquarters of the Seventh Day Adventist Church. Turn right at the narrow road to **Kiulu**, just before the causeway crossing the river in front of Tamparuli. Follow this steep and winding road for about 15 minutes until you see a fairly large village on the river to your left. The road forks just before a bridge; take the left fork over the bridge towards Kiulu (there is no signpost). Continue driving on the main road, passing Kiulu with its pastel-coloured multi-purpose hall and continue past a large school on the left with the sign 'Selamat Datang' (Welcome). Take the road marked 'Jalan Pukak'. You'll know you're on the correct road when you pass the big mosque a moment or so later.

You're now well and truly in Kadazandusun territory, the land of the hill-farming Kadazandusun tribe, hardy folk who have, for

Washday for these Kadazandusun women at Kampung Pukak

generations, planted rice in these rich valleys and on the lower slopes of the Crocker Range. For the next 10–15 minutes, you will drive through glorious scenery with terraced paddy fields, simple farmhouses, giant stands of bamboo, glimpses of the river burbling over smooth stones and spanned by suspension bridges seemingly as frail as a spider's web.

At **Pukak**, a cluster of rough wooden stalls and shops on both sides of the road, take the left-hand fork of the road downhill towards the school ('Sekolah Kebangsaan Pukak, Tuaran') and follow a hairpin bend to the left. Continue down this dirt road for a couple of hundred metres and you'll find yourself in a wide grassy field at the edge of the river, the opposite bank a wall of green rearing up almost vertically. To the left is a suspension bridge and a small wooden hut. Take your time to walk across the suspension bridge, which is remarkably strong despite its often rather alarming swaying motion.

To reach one of Sabah's most gorgeous picnic and camping sites, drive carefully upriver along the flat green field for about 200m (220yds) where, out of sight of the village and shaded by trees and bamboo, you can revel in the beauty of the surroundings. This is often a good spot for birdwatching and to see butterflies. You may also see a local coming down to check his bamboo fish trap wedged between the rocks of the rapids. A little upriver, there are rapids where you can let yourself be tossed by the currents (depending on the amount of water), or you can swim in the deep, clean stretch of river that forms a respite before the next rapid. There may be a few lianas hanging near an outcrop of rocks on the opposite bank, ideal for playing Tarzan (or Jane) before dropping into the deep water below. You may catch sight of a rubber dinghy floating by as a group of tourists raft down the **Kiulu River**, popular for its combination of beauty and relative ease of navigation.

When you can eventually tear yourself away from this site, follow the same route back, turning left as you come off Jalan Kiulu. Just over 1km (½ mile) beyond the major roundabout on the road towards Kota Kinabalu, you'll see the Ny Siun Hap Pottery, right beside the 29km marker. This pottery is well geared up for visitors, and has a wide range of locally made pots and a souvenir shop.

For centuries, Chinese ceramics have been an important trade item in Borneo, and antique jars are treated as priceless heirlooms. Huge traditional jars with embossed dragons are still created at Soon Yii Seng, while other classical Chinese shapes are incised or embossed with Sabahan and Chinese motifs. Although many items are now made in moulds, you can still see men throwing pots on a wheel, and women painstakingly doing the detailed finishing work and decoration.

The way back to Kota Kinabalu (about an hour and a half from Kampung Pukak) is clearly signposted. It is an especially beautiful drive in the late afternoon, when the sun adds a golden glow.

5. Kinabalu Park

Spend the day among what one expert described as 'the richest and most remarkable assemblage of plants in the world' around Park Headquarters on Mount Kinabalu. Join a guided nature walk, and look for pitcher plants and orchids in the Mountain Garden. Note: if you combine this tour with Itinerary 9, you'll need 2–3 days.

Mount Kinabalu, often claimed as the highest mountain in Southeast Asia, is more accurately described as the tallest mountain in the region outside the Himalayas. Its magnificent variety of vegetation is, however, second to none. This fact was confirmed in 2000, when Kinabalu Park was declared Malaysia's first World Heritage site by UNESCO.

Rhododendron javanicum

This itinerary focuses, not on the mountain *(see Itinerary 12)* but the 754-sq km (291-sq mile) **Kinabalu Park** that surrounds the peak. Travel to Kinabalu Park by mini-bus (about 2 hours and RM10), leaving from in front of Kota Kinabalu's Padang, or by shared taxi leaving from the same area (RM15 per person). There's also a bus leaving for Ranau near the Padang at 8am daily, passing the park. Try to leave no later than 8am, and wear comfortable footwear, bring binoculars and a light jacket.

The route to the mountain takes you along a new highway and past Telipok, a pottery centre. Just as the *padi* fields and water buffalo of **Tuaran** district come into view, the road swings right;

An incredible variety of vegetation surrounds Mount Kinabalu

The map labels:

Mount Kinabalu

Kota Kinabalu ★
South China Sea
SABAH
MALAYSIA
SARAWAK
Kuching
KALIMANTAN
Pontianak
Samarinda
Balipapan
INDONESIA
Banjarmasin

1600 m / 1 mile
Victoria Pk. 4094
Lows Pk. 4101
Lows Gully
Donkeys Ears
Ugly 4054
St. Johns Pk. ▲
SisterPk ▲ 4032 ▲ Mushroom Pk.
4096
Sayat Sayat Hut
Kinabalu South 3933
Tunku Abdul Rahman Pk. 3948
Panar Laban Rockface
Gunting Lagadan
Panar Laban Huts
Laban Rata Rest House
Paka Cave
Hostel ■ Burlington
■ Hut
New Hut
Shelter
Helipad
Shelter
Lipsan's Trig
Bypass
Helipad
Shelter
Layang-Layang
x Radio Sabah Transmiter TV Complex
Shelter
Shelter
Kambarangoh Telecoms Station
Cascade Waterfall
Shelter
Carsons Falls
P.W. D. Power Station
Shelter
Bukit Ular
Cave
Helipad
Park Headquarters

400 m / 437 yards
Power Station
Kiau Gap
Cave
Twin Bed Cabins
Nepenthes Villas
Kiau View Trail
Admin. Bldg.
Bukit Tupai
B. Tupai Trail
Liwagu Cave
Cabins
Hostels
Bukit Burong
Silau-Silau Trail
B. Burong Trail
Cave
Restaurant
Headquarters
Liwagu Trail
Helipad
Bundu Tuhan Trail
Ranau
Mempening Trail
Silau Silau Rd.
Kamborangoh Rd.
Liwagu Trail

---

watch on the left for a suspension bridge as you near **Tamparuli** village. This bridge, typical of the hundreds crossing the rivers of Sabah, has been immortalised in a popular Malay song.

The road now begins its winding climb. Try to sit on the left of the bus for panoramic views of terraced gardens carved out of the steep hillsides, and for tantalising glimpses of the summit of Mount Kinabalu and the waterfall.

Nabalu, about 15 minutes before the Park Headquarters, is known for its durian and *tarap* fruit, green and red-skinned bananas, hill rice and wild honey; you can also pick up a typical Kadazandusun hat for half the city price at the stalls or souvenir shops. On market day (Thursdays), the market is thronged with sturdy women carrying over-loaded woven backpacks *(wakid)*.

The mini-bus will take you right up to the entrance of the Kinabalu Park (RM2 entry fee for day visitors). Have a look at the gift shop and perhaps buy one of the very informative, inexpensive publications produced by Sabah Parks to enhance your visit. Wander down the steps to the Kinabalu Balsam restaurant and relax over a drink on the verandah with a good view of the mountain, if it is not shrouded in clouds, and a chorus of birdsong; Mount Kinabalu has around 280 species of birds, some of them found nowhere else in the world.

Pitcher plant

Kinabalu Park encompasses a variety of habitats, ranging from lower montane forest around the **Poring** region (550m/1,804ft) to montane and upper montane forest, with granite slabs leading to the summit (4,093m/13,428ft) denying all but the hardiest forms of life. The summit, often covered by clouds which sweep up with tremendous speed, can reappear just as suddenly. This dramatic peep-show makes its series of jagged peaks all the more awesome when they thrust into your view.

Walk down the road to the Administration Building, behind this three-storied building you'll find the **Mountain Garden** (open daily for 1 hour at 9am, noon and 3pm). In this carefully laid out garden, the labelled collection of plants serves as an excellent introduction to Kinabalu's flora. Watch out particularly for orchids (many of them tiny), pitcher plants and rhododendron. Take the marked trail across the stream, pausing to read the notices and to listen to the sounds of the forest.

You should be back in front of the Administration Building by 11am for the guided nature walk led by one of the Park staff. If there are many visitors, the group walk can become a little frustrating; try to be as close to the guide as possible so you can hear clearly and ask any questions.

The walk would have probably made you very hungry by now, so head for the Administration Building restaurant. Although often very busy with tour groups at lunch time, you can usually find a place in the smaller room on the right, or on the verandah. You can be sure the vegetable dishes are fresh, as they come from surrounding farms. After lunch, check out the information centre.

There are a number of marked trails, but perhaps the prettiest (and easiest) is the **Silau-Silau Trail**, heading towards the **Power Station Road** and note, not Liwagu Cave. Walk down past the Mountain Garden and along the road to the sign 'Bukit Tupai Trail'. Walk down a few metres; don't turn left where you see the small suspension bridge but go right for about 5m (16ft) and just before the bridge leading to the sports hall, turn left and go downhill across the river. At the sign 'Bukit Tupai Trail, Silau-Silau Trail 4 mins, Bukit Tupai Shelter 15 mins', turn left for the Silau-Silau Trail, which meanders through the forest along the sparkling **Silau-Silau River**.

Living in the park are about over 75 species of frogs, 100 species of reptiles and nearly 30 species of fish. As you walk, watch out for butterflies, including the famous black-and-iridescent green Rajah Brooke's Birdwing, tree shrews and squirrels, and a variety of birds. Look closely at the vegetation, for many of the orchids, fungi and other plants are very small, as are most of the frogs and insects. The majority of trees at this altitude are oaks, chestnuts and laurels, although there are also clusters of thorny rattan palms.

Where the Silau-Silau Trail ends at the Power Station Road, you can either backtrack the way you came, or spend about another hour returning via the **Kiau View Trail**, reached by crossing the Power Station Road and walking down until you see the signpost on your right. This trail, which offers a number of fine viewpoints looking over hillside villages, eventually comes back onto the road near Park Headquarters.

Leave Kinabalu Park no later than 4pm, and walk down to the main road to wait for a passing mini-bus or taxi to take you back to Kota Kinabalu. The mini-buses offer a speedier, albeit more hair-raising, trip than the lumbering big buses.

6. Padas River Rafting

As you hurtle through a torrent of water crashing around huge boulders, you may think that rafting on the Padas is the high point of your trip to Sabah. The chance to raft and view the rainforest from tranquil stretches of river makes this trip unmissable.

Most tour operators can arrange rafting trips on the **Padas River**, but it is best to go straight to the established **Diethelm Borneo Expeditions** (tel: 088-263353). During prolonged periods of heavy rain from December to February – which is also the best time to raft since the water levels are high – landslides may make the railway line along the Padas impassable and you will be offered the alternative of rafting in the less exciting **Kiulu River**. If not, you will be picked up around 6.30am for the drive by bus to **Beaufort**, where your rail trip begins. Bring a complete change of clothes, a towel, sunscreen and a pair of gloves, if possible. It's best to wear trainers, shorts and T-shirt during the rafting trip.

During the 1½-hour drive to Beaufort, you'll have ample time to enjoy the picturesque rural scenery near **Papar**, with paddy fields, water buffaloes and slender white egrets. The road then follows the sweep of **Kimanis Bay**, well known for its slices of yellow and red watermelons dangling from the roadside stalls.

When you arrive in Beaufort, there may be time for a quick coffee in one of the old wooden shophouses facing the station. These are built high on stilts to avoid the periodic flooding of the Padas – you may even see a canoe underneath the boardwalk!

There's a 13-seater railcar which leaves Beaufort at 8.25am on week days, but most rafting operators use the slower and less exciting large train – travel by rail is the only way to pass through the gorge. (Apart from a regular service between Tanjung Aru station in Kota Kinabalu, down to Beaufort and on to Tenom, there is a

Fun on the Padas River

Riverside lodge along the Padas

special old diesel train which does a trip down to Papar and back.) The line along Padas Gorge, completed in 1905, formed the only link between the west coast and agriculturally rich interior until the 1960s, when a road was built across the Crocker Range at Sunsuron Pass.

The toytown railcar takes about 1½ hours to reach the starting point of your rafting trip, Kampung Pangi, rattling past isolated hamlets with gardens and orchards maintained by the Murut people native to this area. The lower stretches of the Padas River are rather sluggish, wide and brown with silt. However, as the gorge narrows and cultivation gives way to rainforest, the river – which drains most of southwestern Sabah – protests at its constriction. During periods of heavy rain, walls of water rear up against huge boulders, and form a tumble of chaotic waves as they race across rapids. When the water level is lower, there are still exciting rapids and the prospect of descending the river, as seen from the safety of the railcar, seems less terrifying.

The railcar pauses briefly for you to leave your change of clothing plus all the essentials your tour operator has brought along for lunch at the railway siding of **Kampung Rayoh**, the finishing point of your rafting adventure. Then it's off again, lurching and bumping up the gorge to **Kampung Pangi**. Here, in a pretty outdoor setting beside a *kampung* house where the rafting equipment is stored, you have time for a quick drink and snack provided by the tour company.

Rafters are given life jackets and helmets, then help carry the inflated rafts down to the launching point on the river. After a few simple instructions on how to hold the paddle and advice on certain safety precautions, you are off. When the first rapids arrive, the excitement begins as you guide the raft through the surging water, all the time trying to hold your slippery perch inside the raft. In between rapids, the raft leader will encourage you to tumble overboard for a spot of body rafting, another name for lying flat on your back, supported by your life jacket as you drift blissfully under a brilliant sky. Watch out for dugout canoes or simple wooden boats pulled up on the sandbanks at the river's edge; you may see some of the local lads trying to catch fish with a circular net which they throw into the river. As your confidence increases, each series of rapids becomes more exciting and when, after about 1½ hours, you reach the finishing point, you want to go back and do the trip all over again.

Have a shower back at Diethelm Borneo Expedition's bamboo-walled river lodge at Kampung Rayoh, and sit down to a delicious barbecue lunch to satisfy the raging appetite you're certain to have worked up during the trip.

EXCURSIONS

7. Rungus Longhouse

Your destination today is a longhouse in the northwest of Sabah as a guest of some of Sabah's most traditional people, the Rungus. En route, if you're travelling on a Thursday or Sunday, you have the chance to explore a colourful local weekly market, and enjoy a picnic lunch at a glorious beach.

Until recently, visiting Rungus longhouses in the **Kudat** district was difficult unless you were quite happy to go without modern facilities. Recently, however, an enterprising group of villagers at **Kampung Bavanggazo** built a couple of wood-and-thatch longhouses to receive visitors. Before going, check the availability of rooms first with the Sabah Tourism Promotion Corporation (STPC) office. Local tour operators organise trips with an interpreter, but, if you prefer the pleasures of independent travel, hire a car for this overnight trip and set off with your sunscreen, insect repellent, swimming gear and plenty of film.

If you're travelling on a Sunday, leave by about 8am so that you'll be in **Kota Belud** about an hour later to catch the *tamu* (market) in full swing; on a Thursday, the **Tamparuli** market will give you a glimpse of the commercial and social event of the week.

The road to Kota Belud was once notorious, at least 1½ hours of twisting, tortuous road over the hills of the Crocker Range between Tamparuli and Kota Belud. A new highway, which leaves Tuaran Road just before industrial Inanam on the outskirts of Kota Kinabalu, now enables traffic to reach Kota Belud in about 1 hour. Part of the road climbs a dramatic ridge, but generally it's an easy drive, often past picturesque paddy fields.

Kota Belud is the heartland of the west coast Bajau, originally seafarers from the southern Philippines who settled along Sabah's coasts; they are now respected as buffalo breeders and horsemen. There's been a lot of hype about the Bajau horseman, often referred to as 'Cowboy of the

Rungus man wearing sigar headgear

37

Colourful market day at Kota Belud

East'. While it's true they make a spectacular sight decked out in their finery and mounted on ponies a-jingle with bells and draped with ribbons on festive occasions, don't expect to see Bajau horsemen galloping down the main street of Kota Belud.

Just 50m (54yds) beyond the bridge where the town sign is posted, turn right at the auto and tyre works into the commercial centre. Note the first restaurant on your left as you enter: **Fung Fung**. This is a good place to return after your short tour of Kota Belud to buy your picnic food.

If it's not a Sunday, stroll along the main street between the Esso and Shell stations and turn right at the row of old wooden shophouses. About half-way along this row, you'll find the **Bismillah Restaurant** and some of the best *roti canai* (flaky Indian bread) in Borneo. Pause for a coffee and *roti*, then return to Fung Fung and order some rice or noodles and other dishes to take away *(nasi bungkus)*, and get some cool drinks.

If it's *tamu* day, drive down the main street towards the mosque, then turn right and drive uphill to the roundabout. Follow the signs for the *tamu mingguan*. You'll know you've arrived by the crowds who come to buy, sell and socialise at Sabah's most famous weekly market. Betel-chewing Kadazandusun women squat by piles of tobacco or fresh mountain vegetables, Illanun women with headscarves and sarongs sell brightly coloured conical food covers, while Bajau men haggle over the price of water buffaloes.

Head back past the mosque and follow the signs along the road towards Kota Marudu and Kudat. Soon you'll be crossing the **Tempasuk** plain, a rice-growing area where some of the marshy land has been declared a bird sanctuary and where dozens of birds can be seen at certain times of the year.

As you leave the softwood forest on the gentle hillslopes once covered by magnificent rainforest, watch out for the

Mount Kinabalu forms a backdrop to the Tempasuk Plain

interesting handicraft stalls beside the road, near the (mis-spelt) sign for the boundary of **Kota Marudu** district.

At the Kota Marudu junction, turn left towards **Kudat**; 31km (19 miles) along this road, turn left at Jalan Tinangol, where a sign reads 'Traditional Rungus Longhouse – Kampung Bavanggazo'. You'll come to another sign 1½km (1 mile) down this road; follow it and a few minutes later you'll come to a gentle valley with a cluster of thatch-roofed homes and longhouses. Largely the effort of the enterprising village headman, Maranjak, the two longhouses are a clever combination of tradition and modern comfort. There are 21 rooms, each with a couple of mosquito-netted mattresses on a raised platform. Showers and proper toilets are provided outside. You'll get to sample the local food and rice wine, and enjoy an evening of Rungus dance.

Apart from the chance to see gentle and hospitable Rungus tribespeople going about their daily lives, you can watch handicrafts being made (and buy the result) – the Rungus are renowned as highly skilled artisans who traditionally make colourful necklaces from local plant seeds and clay – go 'jungle trekking', visit the farms and generally immerse yourself into traditional Rungus life. It can be a wonderful experience, and one that is totally different to the longhouses of Sarawak.

At work on the longhouse verandah

But don't forget that lunch you've brought from Kota Belud. After establishing yourself at Kampung Bavanggazo, drive out to the first sign and head straight instead of turning back to the right. You'll soon come to a T-junction where you turn left; about 15 minutes later, you'll reach the fishing village of **Indarasan**, with its picturesque lagoon and long deserted beach where you can swim and picnic under the shady trees. The people here are mainly Illanun, and today still barter their fish for vegetables and fruit grown by the Rungus people.

After an enjoyable afternoon, head back to enjoy the rest of your stay at Kampung Bavanggazo. The next day, if time permits and if you have a four-wheel drive, you could return to Kota Kinabalu via a stunningly beautiful but rough mountain road, which will add another hour to your travelling time. When you reach the Kota Belud mosque, follow the signs for Ranau. After about 15 minutes, the sealed road comes to an end and you start climbing the Crocker Range. You will eventually (many spectacular views later) join up with the road that goes to Kinabalu Park where you may like to spend the night *(see Itineraries 5 and 9)*, or turn right and head back to Kota Kinabalu via Tamparuli.

Rafflesia bloom

8. On the Nature Trail

See the world's biggest flower, picnic and swim amidst a cloud of butterflies, then explore a remarkable collection of rare Borneo orchids and wander about a living museum. Stay overnight in Tenom, riding the quaint rail-car along the dramatic Padas Gorge to return to Kota Kinabalu next day.

For this overnight tour, you'll need either to hire a car, or charter a taxi (around RM200) to take you to Tenom and stay with you until around 5.30pm. Before leaving Kota Kinabalu, call Tenom Railway Station (tel: 087-735514) to book your seats on the 6.30am railcar from Tenom to Beaufort the following morning, and book a night's accommodation at one of the Tenom hotels. Pack swimming gear, mosquito repellent and a picnic lunch (or plan to buy food en route) and leave Kota Kinabalu around 8.30am.

Your first destination is the **Rafflesia Information Centre** (open daily 8am–4pm), located in the **Rafflesia Rainforest Reserve** up in the **Crocker Range**. After passing through Penampang, the road begins its steep climb up sharply ridged mountains, a never-ending sea of green waves flowing down to the coast.

Beyond Kampung Moyog, look to the left for glimpses of **Mount Kinabalu**. Fresh *shiitake* mushrooms are grown in the thatched huts by the road, while isolated farmers raise pineapples, bananas and vegetables which they sell in simple roadside stalls. When you reach the Gunung Emas Highlands Resort, about an hour after leaving Kota Kinabalu, it's time to stop for a coffee and perhaps some of the excellent toasted Chinese dumplings called *woh teh*. Then go to the back of the building to the verandah for a panoramic view of the Crocker Range.

Continue travelling towards the **Sinsuron Pass**, which crosses the range at 1,649m (5,410ft). Within 10 minutes, you should reach the Rafflesia Information Centre on the left, which contains all you could possibly want to know about the amazing flower discovered by Sir Stamford Raffles in 1830 during his first sojourn on the west coast of Sumatra. A para-

Nature Trail
25 km / 15 miles

P. GAYA
Kota Kinabalu
Menggatal
Inanam
Kasigui
Penampang
Gunung Emas
Alab 2084
Kinarut
S. Papar
Rafflesia Centre
South China Sea
Papar
Kayau
Tambunan
Kimanis
Telukan Kimanis
Kg. Ulu Kimanis
Lingan 1386
Bongawan
Kitau
Rinangisan 1325
S. Pegalan
Membakut
Sinalakoi
S. Membakut
Taman Bandukan
Beaufort
Bingkor
Kg. Sinarun Baru
Kg. Senagang
Keningau
Kg. Kadalakan
Malutut 1287
Melalap
S. Pegalan
S. Padas
Sabah Agricultural Park
Kg. Sook
S. Pangi
Tenom

sitic plant whose bloom can grow up to one metre in diameter, the Rafflesia's life cycle takes a whole nine months or more. When in bloom the Rafflesia will only last for about a few weeks, giving off an unpleasant stench when it starts to rot.

A ranger at the Rafflesia Information Centre will be able to tell you if there are any Rafflesias in bloom along the reserve's trails; there are some 20 or so identified plots within the reserve. Take just a few minutes to follow the **Lookout Trail** to the shelter overlooking Sinsuron on the Tambunan plain below. The altitude of around 1,000m (3,280ft) makes hiking very pleasant, and do watch out for orchids on trees and fallen branches.

Continue down the road to Tambunan and if you haven't packed a picnic lunch, buy takeaway Chinese food from the **Restoran Tambunan** next to Sabah Bank. Keep heading south along the highway until the marked turn-off to Bingkor, just before Keningau. At Bingkor's cluster of old wooden shophouses, turn right towards **Taman Bandukan**, a delightful picnic spot by a river renowned for its thousands of butterflies. Pause here for lunch and a splash in the

Sinsuron lookout

stream, and don't be surprised if butterflies land on you.

Drive on through Keningau to **Tenom**, an attractive town in a rich agricultural area where Muruts are the dominant ethnic group. Turn left just before the open playing field, cross the railway line and head for the **Agricultural Research Station** (frequently called – even on signboards – by its old name, Cocoa Research Station). This was originally a research centre for cocoa and rubber, but today it is better known as an important breeding centre for orchids.

The first stage of an agricultural park, **Taman Pertanian Sabah**, opened in late 2000 within the grounds of the research station. Designed to promote agro-tourism as well as to provide recreational and educational facilities, the park promises to be one of Sabah's top attractions. A series of themed

As the sign says

BAHAGIAN PEMELIHARAAN BUNGA ORKID

TENOM ORCHID CENTRE

AGRICULTURAL RESEARCH STATION
LAGUD SEREBANG

A rare native orchid

gardens feature plants such as bamboos, rattans, heliconias and gingers. In addition, there is a garden devoted to beekeeping (with a blaze of flowers to attract the bees and demonstrations of gathering honey), as well as a 'honey museum'. There's another feature on mushroom growing and an impressive 'garden of evolution', showing how plants evolved over the millennia.

The nucleus of the agricultural park, which is open daily from 8am–5pm (RM25 for non-Malaysians), is the **Tenom Orchid Centre**, which began as a research project in 1981, housing the world's biggest collection of native Borneo lowland orchids. The magnificent orchids here range in size from tiny pin heads to cascades of brilliant blooms several metres long. If time permits, go to the **Crop Museum**, where dozens of plants and trees are grouped according to their use: medicines, beverages, oils, perfumes and other products. Opposite the agricultural park and across the Pangkalan River is the interesting and creatively designed **Murut Cultural Centre**, showcasing the culture of its people.

Head back for Tenom, where you part company with your taxi or hired car to spend the night *(see Practical Information, page 89)*. For dinner, try the restaurant at the YNL **Entertainment Centre** just across the Padas River, a 5-minute taxi ride away; their steamed tilapia, a fresh-water fish raised locally, is excellent. Alternatively, enjoy an excellent and moderately priced Chinese dinner at **Chi Hin** at the back of the block opposite Hotel Antanom.

Necklace orchid

Next morning, try to be at the railway station by 6.15am to get a seat in front of the railcar, or on the left-hand side, for the best views. The railway, until recently Tenom's only link with the coast, cuts through a narrow gorge as it follows the **Padas River** *(see Itinerary 6)*. Early morning is the loveliest time to ride the railcar, when the rising mist is caught in the forest canopy and the spiders' webs are strung with diamonds of dew. Birds greet the new day with ecstatic calls, some of them swooping across the river in search of insects.

When you arrive at Beaufort Station about 1½ hours later, cross to the old shophouses opposite for breakfast. A plate of steaming fried noodles and a fragrant local coffee starts off the day.

Take either a mini-bus (RM5) or share a taxi (RM8 per person) for the 1½-hour trip back to Kota Kinabalu.

9. Canopy Walk and Poring Hot Springs

Get a monkey's-eye view from a walkway strung high in the jungle canopy, soak in hot springs and hike to a waterfall at Poring, part of Kinabalu Park. After a night in the mountain cool, revel in the amazingly diverse plant life around Park Headquarters before returning to Kota Kinabalu. Note: For a longer stay, this tour can be combined with Itinerary 5.

As there is no regular transport service between Poring and Kinabalu Park Headquarters, it's easiest to either hire a car for this two-day trip, or charter a taxi to stay with you until the first day's evening (you can return by mini-bus the following day). As you will be spending the night in the **Kinabalu Park**, it is essential to book accommodation in advance *(see Practical Information, page 88)*. Pack a swimming costume and towel for the hot springs and leave by about 7.30am for Ranau. (Avoid doing this trip on a Sunday, when Poring is extremely busy with local visitors.)

Follow the route up to **Mount Kinabalu** *(see Itinerary 5)*. About 5km (3 miles) past the entrance to Kinabalu Park, you'll see the important agricultural district of **Kundasang**, a clutter of ramshackle stalls offering a range of mountain produce. This market is very popular with visitors from Kota Kinabalu, who stock up on fresh cabbages, cauliflower, asparagus, mushrooms and flowers. Kundasang is also home to a war memorial honouring both local civilians and armed forces who died during the Japanese Occupation. In **Ranau**, a much simpler memorial (a cairn of stones topped by a green-painted helmet) was erected by the Australian Armed Forces, in memory of the almost 2,400 prisoners of war who died on a march from Sandakan during the final days of the Japanese Occupation (there were just six survivors).

Follow the signs for **Poring Hot Springs** (Air Panas), 27km (17

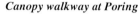

Canopy walkway at Poring

Death March memorial at Ranau

miles) along a sealed road from Ranau. At Poring, located in the eastern part of Kinabalu Park, there's an entrance fee. Attractions here, apart from the hot springs themselves, and a series of freshwater fun pools with a water slide, include a Canopy Walkway, the first of its kind in the region, which offers a bird's-eye view of the rainforest from a walkway suspended between giant trees. Open daily 9am–4pm. To reach the walkway, you take a track 800m (875yds) up a steep hillside, but the walkway itself is easy, provided you don't suffer from vertigo.

Poring also has a Tropical Garden (open daily for 1 hour at 1.30pm) with some superb flowers and shrubs, while orchid enthusiasts should not miss the Orchid Conservation Centre (open daily 2.30pm).

Don't forget to relax in a tub of hot mineral water. The baths, originally built during the Japanese Occupation, are set in glorious surroundings – stands of enormous *poring* bamboo which gives this area its name, hibiscus, fruit trees, palms and even pine trees. Pluck up your courage and enjoy a sauna-like effect, going straight from a soak in the hot mineral water into the cold water of the landscaped rock pool nearby. When you've finished, enjoy lunch in the restaurant near the baths.

Decide how to spend your afternoon: there are several marked trails you can follow (most fairly steep), to waterfalls and to a tumble of boulders known as the Bat Cave, where bats spend the day hanging upside down. If you feel energetic, take the 1½-hour trek to

Poring Hot Springs: take a refreshing dip in the landscaped rock pool

the lovely **Langanan Waterfall**. Since few visitors come here, you're more likely to see wildlife such as monkeys and squirrels.

You might decide to concentrate on butterflies and the iridescent dragonflies that can be seen around the hot baths and trickles of mineral-rich water nearby. The **Taman Kupu Kupu** (Butterfly Park; open daily 9am–4pm) is like a huge aviary where you can observe hundreds of live butterflies as well as a number of spectacular insects, including huge rhinoceros beetles and 20-cm (8-inch) long stick insects. Taman Kupu Kupu has at least 30 species of butterflies from the Poring region; one of the most spectacular is the vivid yellow-and-black

Common Birdwing. Butterflies are most active during bright sunlight; if the day happens to be cloudy, just wait for the sun (and the butterflies) to reappear.

Drive to Kinabalu Park Headquarters for a relaxing night, with the fresh mountain air to whet your appetite. The **Liwagu Cafeteria** in the Kinabalu Park's Administration Building offers a range of good local as well as Western food; although crowded with tour groups at lunch time, it is a pleasant place to eat at night. For a very different view of the forest, go for a night walk with a torch along one of the trails. Look closely on and under the leaves for stick insects, ranging from about 4cm (1½inch) up to a giant 30cm (12 inch). You might also spot luminous fungi and the tiny frogs common to Kinabalu.

The next day, get up early in the morning for a walk along the roads near Park Headquarters to spot the hundreds of birds intent on awakening the whole

A Butterfly Park resident

world with their constant chirping. Breathe in the bracing mountain air over breakfast on the verandah of the **Kinabalu Balsam Restaurant** (near the Park entrance) then wander down to the **Mountain Garden** (open daily for 1 hour at 9am, noon and 3pm) for an introduction to the flora of Kinabalu Park. Watch out particularly for the carnivorous pitcher plants, whose leaves are adapted into a cup where hapless insects are digested. If you're lucky, the rare slipper orchid may be in bloom.

If you're not in a hurry, stroll along one of the nature trails, such as the **Silau-Silau Trail**, before driving back or catching a mini-bus to Kota Kinabalu outside the Kinabalu Park Headquarters.

Fly or drive to Sandakan on the east coast. The following day, see conservation in action at the orang-utan sanctuary in Sepilok, then visit caves where birds' nests that pleased the palates of Chinese emperors are still gathered. Drift through the swamp forest for an intimate close-up of proboscis monkeys. Spend the night in a lodge on the banks of the Kinabatangan River before returning to Sandakan, or continue with Itinerary 11.

You can do this entire trip with a tour operator, but if you have the time, it is far more pleasurable to hire your own transport and make a leisurely three-day trip.

Be sure to arrange your stay at Sukau, on the banks of the Kinabatangan River, before leaving Kota Kinabalu. Recommended east coast operators include Sipadan Dive Centre (088-240584) and Wildlife Expeditions (088-254300 or 089-219616). Before you leave, pack binoculars, sunscreen and a hat; an umbrella is also handy in case of afternoon showers. Try also to pick up a copy of the small but informative book *Orang-utan: Malaysia's Mascot (see Practical Information, page 95).*

Fly to **Sandakan** on the east coast from Kota Kinabalu, making sure you request a window seat on the left side of the plane for the best views. Or else, hire a car and drive the 5-hour, 364-km (226-mile) journey to Sandakan, pausing along the way at Kinabalu Park *(see Itinerary 5).* Stay the night in Sandakan, capital of British North Borneo until 1946 and one of the main centres of Sabah's

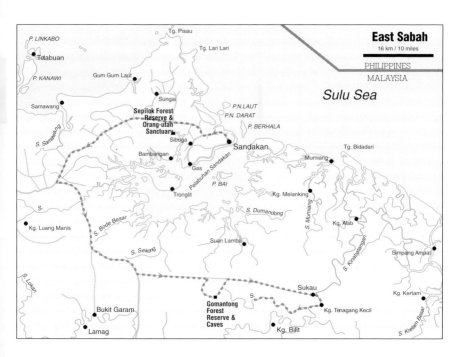

Kinabatangan River

timber industry. For a stunning view of the town and bay by night, as well as a superb seafood meal, drive up to **Trig Hill** and dine in the courtyard of the first Chinese restaurant on the steep ridge.

The following morning, if you prefer not to have breakfast in your hotel, you might like to try *coto makassar*, a beefy Indonesian soup with chunks of rice cake, at one of the coffee shops such as **Hap Seng** near Sandakan market. Alternatively, **Fairwood Restaurant** in Jalan Tiga (almost opposite Kentucky Fried Chicken) offers a range of inexpensive local food for breakfast. Hire a car if you don't have one already, and set off for Sepilok.

Set in 43 sq km (16 sq miles) of virgin rainforest just 25km (15 miles) from Sandakan, the **Sepilok Orang-utan Sanctuary** was begun in 1964 to help motherless baby orang-utans, usually caught during logging operations or by illegal hunting, to learn to live in the wilds again. The Wildlife Department permits visitors to observe the twice-daily feeding at Sepilok in order to promote an interest in their conservation efforts.

Playful orang-utan babies

Try to arrive at the Sanctuary by about 9.30am and, after registering and paying the entrance fee, enjoy a leisurely stroll along the boardwalk to the feeding platform. Along the way, you may see very young orang-utans literally learning the ropes as they are encouraged by park rangers to develop

47

Gomantong Caves

confidence and the skills that will eventually enable them to survive in the rainforest.

At the feeding platform, orang-utans still learning to adjust to the forest are given a ration of milk and bananas at 10am and 3pm daily. Watch out also for the cheeky macaque monkeys, which will come right up to your viewing platform.

After enjoying the orang-utans, stop to watch the interesting video presentation at the information centre before heading along **Labuk Road**, the main route to Kota Kinabalu as well as leading to the turn-off to Lahad Datu and then to **Gomantong** and **Sukau**. The busy junction of the Lahad Datu road is still known to the locals as Mile 32. Pause for lunch in one of the restaurants here: Malay food at the outlet on the corner, and Chinese food at any of

48

the restaurants opposite on the main road. Alternatively, ask the restaurant to pack your food and drinks and take them with you to enjoy at the picnic tables at Gomantong.

From the Mile 32 junction, take the road towards Lahad Datu for 48km (30 miles) until you come to the turn-off to your left for Sukau. Follow the untarred road for 23km (14 miles) until you see the sign on the right for **Gomantong Forest Reserve** (open daily 8am–4.15pm).

The reserve, roughly the same size as Sepilok, is famed for the edible nests built by swifts on the walls of its limestone caves. The Gomantong reserve is also a good area for birdwatching, and, at certain times of year, clouds of butterflies. Harvesting of the birds' nests is strictly controlled by the Wildlife Department to avoid excessive exploitation. Twice a year, for a period of about two weeks, workers risk life and limb to climb flimsy rattan ladders as tall as 60m (196ft) from the cave floor to ceiling. Gingerly, the workers inch their way along bamboo poles to gather the nests stuck to the roofs of the caves.

The harvesting season varies, but generally the periods March to April and August to September are the times when the nests are collected. Although a visit is obviously more spectacular during harvesting, the limestone caves are impressive at any time of year. Bats also frequent the caves, so the boardwalk is carpeted with a thick layer of guano housing thousands of beetles and other insects; wear sensible footwear.

Two varieties of swiftlet make edible nests of saliva at Gomantong: the ones made of swiftlet saliva mixed with feathers are found in the so-called 'black' caves, while the more expensive nests (which can fetch US$500 a kilo when cleaned of their bits of grit and feathers) of pure saliva are found in the less accessible 'white' caves. Prized by the Chinese, the dried saliva is believed to cure a host of ailments from acne to asthma.

An intrepid nest gatherer

It's about a 25-minute drive from Gomantong to **Sukau**, a village on the banks of Sabah's biggest river, the Kinabatangan. If you're staying at the lodges run by SI Tours or Discovery Tours, you can park your car right in front of the lodge. Alternatively, you can park near one of the village houses (there is a small fee) and take a short boat ride to one of the other lodges along the Kinabatangan River.

Wherever you're staying, you'll need to be ready by about 3.30–4pm to set off by small boat to explore the **Kinabatangan River** and head up a tributary, the **Menanggol River**. As you motor slowly up this narrow river, it's like being in a tiny country lane after the highway of the Kinabatangan. You're an inseparable part of the environment, surrounded by mangroves and within intimate distance of an Oriental Darter which knifes into the water, or a mangrove snake coiled in the branches.

Provided there are not too many other tourists on the Menanggol, you might see a number of bird species along the river. With a copy of *Pocket Guide to the Birds of Borneo, (see Practical Information, page 95)* you'll be able to identify the hornbills often seen flapping noisily overhead, the Storkbilled Kingfisher with gleaming enamel-blue wings, or the dramatic ruby-and-jet-black Broadbill with his unusual pale blue beak and whiskers. If you're not already a confirmed birdwatcher, be prepared to be converted by this matchless display of feathered beauties.

As the day cools, proboscis monkeys, found only on the island of Borneo, start to congregate in their favourite *Sonneratia* trees along the river banks. Once described as 'the grotesque honker of the Borneo swamps', male proboscis monkeys have a nose Jimmy Durante would envy, and a huge pot belly. They leap with insane abandon, crash-landing noisily in the trees, and thanks to webbed feet, can even swim. If you come

A surprisingly sedate proboscis monkey

across a family of proboscis monkeys, you may see a mother anxiously protecting her baby; the much smaller females have a more refined appearance with delicately uptilted noses, and are far less exhibitionist in their behaviour.

Owing to disturbance of their habitat by the establishment of oil palm plantations, elephants (found nowhere else in Borneo) may sometimes be seen in groups along the Kinabatangan River. A WWF-funded project to protect the Kinabatangan wetlands is currently underway so that this fragile environment and its inhabitants will be preserved. From Sukau, you can either return to Kota Kinabalu or travel on to the Turtle Islands Marine Park at Pulau Selingan to watch nesting sea turtles *(Itinerary 11)*.

50

A green turtle laying eggs

11. Turtle Islands Marine Park

Experience conservation in action at remote Pulau Selingan as you watch the green turtle dragging herself ashore at night to lay her eggs. When the protected eggs are hatched, the baby turtles are carefully returned to the sea, something which you can assist in if you don't mind the tiny creatures scrabbling all over your feet as they race for the ocean.

Fly or drive to **Sandakan** on the east coast from Kota Kinabalu if you didn't do *Itinerary 10*. It is not necessary to use a tour operator to visit **Turtle Islands Marine Park** for this overnight tour, but you must book the very limited accommodations available at **Pulau Selingan** (one of the three islands that make up the park) at Crystal Quest Sdn Bhd, tel: 089-212711, email: cquest@tm.net.my. They also arrange for the return boat trip. The best time to visit is between April and October, when the turtles converge on the islands, and the southwest monsoon makes the boat trip more comfortable. Bring a swimming costume, sunscreen, insect repellent and torch with you.

Start the day by having breakfast in one of the coffee shops or Indian-Muslim restaurants opposite the **Sandakan market**. You might like to buy some fruit and snacks in the market, as the restaurant on Pulau Selingan is limited and naturally more expensive. Travel by taxi (RM3–5) to the jetty where you've arranged with Sabah Parks to meet your boat.

The boat trip should take about 1 hour, depending on the condition of the waters. You'll pass the nearby island of **Berhala**, once a leper colony and then a prisoner-of-war camp. The coastline is eventually left behind as you head towards the three 'Turtle Islands', Selingan, Bakungan Kecil and Gulisan, purchased by the state government in 1971 to ensure their status as protected turtle sanctuaries.

Poaching of the turtle eggs – which fetch around RM1 each in the local markets – was a serious problem for many years in Sabah, compounded by the proximity of the Philippine islands, where turtle eggs are considered a delicacy. In order to protect the turtles and their eggs, armed police reinforce the work of Sabah Park rangers by patrolling the islands.

On arrival at Selingan, you'll have the rest of the day to swim

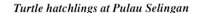
Turtle hatchlings at Pulau Selingan

Survival of the fittest: racing to see who hits the water first

in the clear waters, walk around the island (a 30-minute exercise) or just relax. After watching the sunset, have a look at the hatchery, where baby turtles, after a gestation period of 50–60 days, should now be emerging in the evening cool from the sand into a netted enclosure.

After dinner, wait in your chalet for a ranger to call you when the turtles waddle up the beach to lay their eggs. It is vital not to disturb the amphibians with bright lights or noise, so crouch quietly in the warm night as you watch a huge shape drag herself laboriously up the beach to begin digging a pit with her flippers. She will pause frequently to give an almost human sigh before continuing her exhausting task. When the pit is ready, the turtle will squat over it and lay 100 or more eggs resembling soft-shelled ping-pong balls. As she begins to cover the eggs, the ranger will tag her and lift her to one side before scooping the eggs into a bucket. Being a creature of habit, the mother turtle will persist in covering the now empty pit before dragging herself back to the sea.

Follow the ranger back to the hatchery, where he'll bury the newly laid eggs, tagging the spot with a marker indicating the date and number of eggs. Then it's time to carry the hatchlings that have just emerged from the sand into their protected enclosure to the water's edge. If you ask, the ranger will let you help in this exciting task, but be warned: as you tip the baby turtles out of the

Incubating eggs

bucket onto the sand, they tickle like crazy as they run over your feet, scattering in all directions before being guided by a torch beam and some deep instinct into the sea.

During the height of the laying season, more than a dozen turtles may drag themselves onto the beaches of Pulau Selingan during the course of an evening. Each time, the rangers repeat their performance, gathering and reburying the eggs in the hatchery. It is estimated that only 30 percent of the baby turtles released into the sea survive to adulthood. By some still unexplained phenomenon, female turtles, on maturity, will return to the very beach where they themselves were hatched to lay their eggs.

Have an early breakfast and return to Sandakan. If you have the time, consider doing *Itinerary 10* if you haven't already, before flying or driving back to Kota Kinabalu.

12. Mount Kinabalu

All of north Borneo lies at your feet as you triumphantly stand on Low's Peak, 4,093m (13,428ft) above the South China Sea. The highest peak in the region outside of the Himalayas and the second tallest in Southeast Asia, Mount Kinabalu is a magnet that no visitor in good physical condition should resist.

Many climbers attempt the trip from Kota Kinabalu to the summit and back in just two days. It can, of course, be done (the fastest man up to the summit and back to Park Headquarters did it in less than three hours) but why push yourself so hard when there's so much to be enjoyed? The following three-day itinerary is ideal: the first day is spent around Park Headquarters at 1,500m (4,921ft), acclimatising to the altitude; the second day is spent climbing at a leisurely pace to the accommodation up at **Panar Laban** (3,352m/ 10,997ft)); and finally on the third day, you make for the summit, returning to Park Headquarters and then back down to Kota Kinabalu or to spend the night relaxing at **Poring Hot Springs** first.

Laban Rata rest house

The summit at last

Book your accommodation in advance at Kinabalu Nature Resorts *(see Practical Information, page 88)*. Before leaving Kota Kinabalu, make sure you have warm clothing; the temperature can fall below zero on the summit. Trainers are preferable to heavy boots, and a change of socks should be brought as the track is often wet. Gloves are essential for grasping the ropes on the granite slopes. A light plastic raincoat or poncho can be useful, and many climbers swear an umbrella is indispensable. You will not need to carry water on the first day, as it's available at every rest point; however, a half-litre plastic bottle of water for drinking at the summit is recommended. Chocolate and biscuits can be bought at Kinabalu Balsam Restaurant at Park Headquarters; if you want apples and nuts, buy them before leaving Kota Kinabalu. Painkillers to cope with any discomfort caused by the altitude are also recommended.

It is commonly claimed that **Mount Kinabalu** is one of the world's easiest mountains to climb. True, it doesn't require any mountaineering skills, and the well maintained trail follows the line of least resistance all the way up. But make no mistake: the climb is extremely strenuous, taxing both your legs and lungs. If you're

View from the summit plateau

Ever onwards and upwards

planning an ascent well in advance, it's worth embarking on a regular excercise programme to make sure you're really fit for the climb.

If you're carrying a heavy pack, you may find the Ranau bus, which departs at 8am from near the north end of the Padang, gives you more room. Otherwise, take one of the Ranau mini-buses in front of the Padang for the 2-hour, RM10 trip to Kinabalu Park.

Register when you arrive at **Kinabalu Park**, then spend the rest of the day familiarising yourself with the mountain. Check the exhibit centre at the Administration Building for interesting historical and botanical information, and aerial photos of the mountain. You'll learn that geologically speaking, Mount Kinabalu is a mere babe, its summit shaped by the last ice age 10,000 years ago, and is still growing. You'll also discover that the mountain is host to species of plants, birds and small animals found nowhere else in the world.

Visit the **Mountain Garden** for a taste of what you're likely to encounter as you climb, with such strikingly different plants as rat-

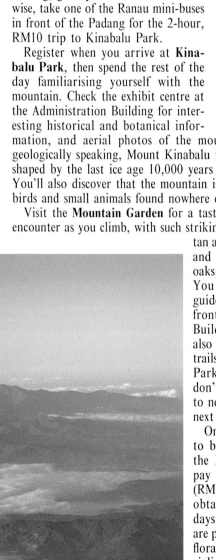

tan and rhododendron, bamboo and buttercups, orchids and oaks, pitcher plants and violets. You might like to join the guided nature walk starting in front of the Administration Building at 11am. You could also explore one of the marked trails – try **Silau-Silau** – around Park Headquarters, though don't overdo it – you're going to need all your energy for the next day.

On the second day, be sure to be at the office just inside the Park entrance by 7am to pay for your climbing permit (RM50 for non-Malaysians) and obtain a guide (RM50 for 2 days for 1–3 persons). If you are particularly interested in the flora of the park, ask for a specialist guide. Take a pick-up or Park bus (RM10 per person) to the Power Station (otherwise a

55

Stunning Low's Rhododendron

1-hour walk) where you begin your climb. The earlier you start, the better, as weather conditions can often deteriorate in the afternoon.

As you leave the lower montane forest, you'll notice changes in the vegetation as you enter a dense, cool kingdom where thick moss drips from the trees, and where climbing bamboos and tree-ferns crowd together. At each rest stop, don't miss the interesting information panels. Some of the 25 species of rhododendron found on the mountain may be in bloom in the high level moss forest; watch out for the spectacular golden *Rhododendron lowii*, or the orange *R. javanicum*. At around 2,700m (8,858ft), a change in soil causes a dramatic difference, with much more open vegetation which is home to the carnivorous pitcher plants *(Nepenthes)*. Around 3,000m (9,842ft), and getting closer to the end of today's climb, the trees seem to shrink, their tortured limbs twisted by the wind.

By the time **Laban Rata Rest House** comes into view, you'll be able to gaze at the uncompromising granite bulk of the summit looming above you, its harsh stone slabs denying life to all but the most tenacious of plants clinging to tiny pockets of soil. Enjoy your well-earned rest, a good meal, and maybe even a short snooze before wandering down to the helipad for a glorious view of the sunset (weather permitting of course).

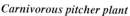

Carnivorous pitcher plant

The combination of food and high altitude makes many people feel nauseous, so limit yourself to a hot drink and take chocolate, nuts and fruit (not forgetting your half-litre bottle of water) to the summit. Your guide will try to persuade you to get up at 2am for an early breakfast and a 3am departure for the summit. The guides are convinced that every climber has a burning desire to see the sunrise from the summit. If you don't mind pulling yourself by rope up a granite rock face while trying to hold your torch in the dark, freezing in the pre-dawn cold, then queueing up with other climbers to stand on the summit, follow the guide's advice. Or do as I do, and leave at 5am so that by the time you're scaling the first granite face, you no longer need a torch and have both hands free for the rope. You'll be warmed by the rising sun as you reach the most exposed portion of the mountain, which can be bitterly cold before dawn. As you finally approach **Low's Peak** (2 hours from Laban Rata), all the other climbers are on their way down and you'll have the summit to yourself.

The first man to reach this peak (in 1888) was botanist John Whitehead, naming it after Hugh Low, who had climbed the mountain in 1851 but, owing to a broken altimeter, failed to find the true summit. On a clear day, the views from this tiny peak are stunning, with the forested hills, rivers, estuaries and coastline lay sprawled far below. Equally breathtaking is the awesome 1,800m (5,905ft) chasm of **Low's Gully**, which virtually splits the mountain in two.

In 1994, a group led by British army officers underestimated the challenges of Low's Gully. Unable to find an exit after lowering themselves down into the gully by rope, they were forced to spend several days there before being rescued by helicopter.

When you can finally tear yourself away from the wondrous views on the summit, retrace your steps to the Laban Rata Rest House, have breakfast and a rest for a while before going back down to Park Headquarters. If time allows, you can stay for another day, resting and exploring the surroundings before the descent.

You can purchase a certificate to prove you've made the summit, though your aching legs are going to remind you of that fact constantly for the next couple of days. Take a mini-bus back to Kota Kina-

Kinabalu's highest growing orchids

balu or, if you can spare another day, go on to Poring Hot Springs (part of Kinabalu Park) if you haven't already *(see Itinerary 9)* to treat yourself to a relaxing soak in the hot tubs. You'll certainly need it after the climb up Mount Kinabalu. Stay overnight in one of the hostels or chalets. Be sure to arrange with the mini-bus or taxi which brought you to Poring to pick you up the following day to return to the city.

13. Sipadan and Layang Layang

Two outstanding dive sites – Sipadan, an oceanic island in the Celebes Sea and Layang Layang, a remote atoll far off Sabah's west coast in the South China Sea – offer scuba divers an unrivalled view of the marine riches of this region.

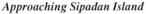

Pulau Sipadan, a 12-hectare (30-acre) dot in the ocean, became internationally renowned after Borneo Divers opened their first simple dive lodge in 1989. Fringed by coral and with a 600-metre (1,970-ft) drop to the ocean floor, Sipadan has it all: beautiful hard and soft corals, underwater caves, a myriad of brilliantly coloured reef fish, dozens of sea turtles (many of which nest on the beaches) and big pelagic fish including sharks, schooling barracudas and jacks.

Uncontrolled development of this superb dive spot finally led to government intervention in mid-1999, when strict quotas were introduced on the number of guests permitted to stay on Sipadan, and the number of divers permitted to visit from nearby resorts. Mabul island and Kapalai reef both offer alternative accommodation to Sipadan, but divers should check in advance that they will be able to dive at Sipadan.

Soft corals are aplenty

Pulau Sipadan hit the world's headlines in 2000, when a party of divers and several staff members were kidnapped by a group of Filipino Muslim rebels calling themselves Abu Saayaf, and held for four months in the southern Philippines. Armed police and navy patrols have since been introduced, and divers are now back in full force to experience some of the world's most remarkable diving.

Dive operators offer packages which include a 40-minute flight

Approaching Sipadan Island

Sipadan's waters teem with turtles

from Kota Kinabalu to Tawau, then a 1½-hour road journey to Semporna followed by a 45-minute speedboat ride.

Sabah's most remote dive site is, ironically, the quickest to reach. **Layang Layang** atoll, located on the Borneo Banks not far from the Spratly Islands in the South China Sea, is just over 1 hour by light plane from Kota Kinabalu. Until early 1990, Layang Layang was known as Swallow Reef and was a mere strip of exposed coral and sand on one edge of a ring of coral surrounding a shallow lagoon. A small island was created for a Malaysian Navy base (discreetly located at one end), with a Kuala Lumpur-based company given sole rights to run a luxurious dive resort, opened in 1995.

Thanks to its remote location more than 200km off the coast, Layang Layang offers stunning visibility with absolutely no pollution whatsoever. During April and May, schools of hammerhead sharks can be seen, and throughout the year, divers might spot manta rays, dolphins, grey tip reef sharks, leopard sharks, turtles and large fish such as wrasse, barracuda and trevally.

Not only is the diving excellent, the resort itself offers almost indecent comfort with air-conditioned rooms and all the facilities of a city hotel, a very good restaurant, a large swimming pool, and a few games. At night, divers can watch (and purchase, if they like) videos of their dive filmed by Scubazoo.

Another attraction here is the thousands of birds (mostly sooty terns, masked terns and brown noddys) which nest at one end of the island. They arrive around May or June, begin their courtship rituals, mate, lay eggs directly on the ground and remain until their hatchlings are big enough to leave. This impressive sight is enough to convert any diver into a bird watcher.

Sooty terns nesting at Layang Layang

Segama River in Danum rainforest

14. Danum Valley Conservation Area

Discover the lowland tropical rainforest, the world's most complex ecosystem, in the comfort of the Borneo Rainforest Lodge.

Book accommodation in advance *(see Practical Information, page 91)* and arrange your return flight to **Lahad Datu**, on Sabah's east coast. Most visitors prefer to take the 6.25am flight from Kota Kinabalu (sit on the left of the plane for a view of Mount Kinabalu en route), and are met on arrival at Lahad Datu by staff of Borneo Rainforest Lodge. There's time for a quick breakfast in one of the coffee shops before setting out on the 2-hour drive to the 438-sq km (170-sq mile) **Danum Valley Conservation Area**, where the **Borneo Rainforest Lodge** is located. Be sure to ask one of the staff for the background leaflet that includes a map of your route and interesting information on the area you will be driving through.

Established in 1986 as a centre for conservation, research and education, the conservation area is the home of the **Danum Valley Field Centre**, one of the leading tropical rainforest research and environmental education centres in Southeast Asia. The success of this centre led to the opening, in 1994, of the Borneo Rainforest Lodge. Built of local timber and river stones, the main building of the lodge is where you'll be welcomed with a drink on arrival. Your accommodation – comfortable and environmentally friendly – will be in one of the bungalows facing the **Danum River**, with magnificent forest-covered hills rearing straight up before you.

The ecologist in charge will discuss your areas of interest and suggest an itinerary. Three days is the minimum you'll need to explore the area without feeling rushed.

Try and follow the patterns of the wildlife in the rainforest, making the most of the cooler morning hours, hauntingly lovely as the mist hangs in the treetops, and venturing out again after 3pm. Mid-afternoon is a good time for one of the easy trails, such as the

60

Segama Trail or the **Sapa Berbandir Trail**. On the way, your guide will point out things that might easily escape the untrained eye: a vivid green Oriental Whipsnake coiled on a leaf; a pill millipede rolling itself into a ball; a tiny orchid; the cry of an Argus pheasant or a leech waiting for you to become a blood donor.

Or he may take you up the **Coffin Trail**, which winds through the forest to end at a cliff face with a stunning view over the forest and the lodge. An ancient Kadazandusun burial site, complete with hardwood coffins and a ceramic jar, was discovered on this cliff face; remnants of a coffin remain in place. The cliff face is an excellent spot for birdwatching, as you are on the same level as the treetops. Spotting animals requires luck and patience. A sudden flick of a tail might alert you to the presence of a pigmy squirrel. You may also spot an unused orang-utan nest; these primates bend the smaller branches in the tree they've chosen for the night and line them with twigs and leaves. Some people have spent hours along the trails and seen nothing, only to be met by three leaf monkeys or a bearded pig along the main road metres from the lodge.

The birdlife is wonderfully rich, with all eight of Sabah's hornbill species found here. One of the best places for birdwatching is the canopy walkway, strung between giant dipterocarp forest, the tallest rainforest in the world. It is easy to spend at least two hours up here, catching sight of a woodpecker drilling a tree trunk, or learning the different calls of the various hornbills.

Prolific fungi

For another perspective of the forest, go on a night drive and see how many creatures you can spot, their eyes shining in the beam of a spotlight: you may see barking deer, civet cats and even wild elephants

Be sure to visit the aptly named **Jacuzzi Pool**, preferably late morning when the sunlight dapples the exquisite jungled glade where a stream tumbles down into a cool, clear pool. Swim here among the tiny fish, listening to all the noises of the forest.

If you can, try to visit the **Field Centre**, 35km (22 miles) away, where you can learn about the current research projects and the problems and potential solutions of maintaining the world's tropical rainforests.

Shopping

The most complete range of souvenirs, handicrafts and gift items – both Sabahan goods and items from Peninsular Malaysia – are found at the big shopping malls in Kota Kinabalu, and Kinabalu National Park. More adventurous shoppers should make a beeline for the Filipino Market and the local *tamu* (weekly market), where you might spot more unusual buys.

What to Buy

Antiques: Genuine Sabahan antiques are difficult to find, although you may be lucky and unearth something at the Gaya Street Fair on Sunday morning. Antiques and handicrafts from Sarawak and Kalimantan are available at some of the bigger shops in Kota Kinabalu.

Basketware: One of Sabah's best buys, ranging from conical Bajau food covers, finely woven Rungus reedwork to carrying baskets and hats made by the Murut and Kadazandusun people.

Beads: Occasionally, valuable antique beads can be purchased, but you're more likely to find brightly coloured necklaces, belts and other items made by Rungus women from modern plastic beads.

Mats: Handwoven mats made from pandanus leaf and other soft grasses are a speciality of the Bajaus.

Kadazan woven backpacks (wakid)

Dastar: Intricately woven cloth squares, usually with geometric designs, *dastar* are folded and worn as headresses by Kadazandusun, Rungus, Illanun and Bajau men.

Pottery: There are several potteries on the outskirts of Kota Kinabalu, producing domestic items as well as ornamental pieces. The latter are usually incised with traditional motifs and glazed.

Sabah mushrooms: Buy home a bag of the fresh brown mushrooms usually known by their Japanese name of *shiitake*. Available from the Central Market or at the outlet in Kota Kinabalu Airport.

Sompoton: This Kadazandusun musical instrument is made from several bamboo tubes with a dried gourd at the base. Distinctively Sabahan.

Weaving: The Rungus women have long been renowned for a type of fabric woven on a backstrap loom. Full length skirts are seldom made today, but it is possible to find smaller cloth rectangles *(dastars)* as well as strips that can be worn as belts or incorporated in cushion covers or clothes.

Where to Buy

Wisma Merdeka, **Komplex Karamunsing** and **Centrepoint** in Kota Kinabalu offer a wide range of shops. Bargaining is not the normal practice in stores located in shopping complexes where prices are marked, although if you buy a number of items at one time you might be able to have the overall price reduced.

The Sunday morning Gaya Street Fair is well worth a visit. You may be lucky enough to pick up a rare antique piece, or at least a good imitation. Watch out for pickpockets. For antiques, gift items and souvenirs, try the following:

BORNEO BOOKS
Ground Floor, Wisma Merdeka
This shop has possibly the best selection of books in Sabah including obscure and difficult to get publications. They also stock a range of pewterware.

BORNEO CRAFT
BG 26, Ground floor, Wisma Merdeka, Phasa II, Jalan Tun Razak
Good selection of local and other Malaysian items.

BORNEO HANDICRAFT
Lot A148, 1st floor, Wisma Merdeka, Jalan Tun Razak
Wide selection of local handicrafts and souvenirs, including the best range of pottery to be found anywhere.

KOMPLEX KARAMUNSING
2nd and 3rd levels
Several shops sell a range of quality handicrafts, some of which are used as household items. Among the best selection of local handicrafts in Kota Kinabalu.

Eating Out

Sabah's magnificent array of seafood – succulent scallops, giant prawns and lobsters, moon-white squid, glistening fresh fish and meaty crabs – is matched only by its veritable cornucopia of tropical fruits and vegetables, as well as temperate climate produce from the slopes of Mount Kinabalu.

The indigenous dishes range from the fish-oriented diet of the coastal Bajau, Suluk and Idahan peoples to jungle produce – wild pig, deer, river fish, ferns and other wild vegetables – of the interior folk such as the Kadazandusun and Murut. It is not easy to find traditional Sabahan food in restaurants and food stalls as most of these are dominated by Chinese, Malay, Indian and Indonesian chefs, many of whom are relatively recent arrivals and whose food has been enthusiastically adopted by the ethnic Sabahans.

Those who enjoy other Asian cuisines need not go hungry: there are Japanese, Thai, Chinese and Korean, even Singaporean chicken rice restaurants. The increasing number of international hotels is bringing in western food and good new restaurants with luxurious surroundings. Continental, Italian, and English fare as well as the ubiquitous American fast food outlets are readily available in Kota Kinabalu's major shopping complexes.

Popular Local Dishes

Some of the dishes you are likely to see in local restaurants, coffee shops and food stalls include:

Banana leaf curry: no, you don't eat the leaves, but the tasty Southern Indian vegetable, fish, chicken or meat curries that are served on freshly cut banana leaf. You can sometimes order *dosai*, wafer-thin rice and lentil flour pancakes eaten with savoury dips.

Barbecued seafood: don't miss this treat of fish, squid or prawns, bathed with a spicy sauce, wrapped in banana leaf and grilled over glowing charcoal.

Chicken rice: A Hainanese favourite which is simple but delicious; tender chicken served with rice, cucumber, soup and a savoury chilli-ginger side dish.

Coto (pronounced 'choto') **makassar**: a robust Indonesian beef soup with chunks of rice cake, and spiced with chilli.

Dim sum: steamed or deep fried titbits usually served at breakfast; stuffed white buns with roasted pork *(char siew pow)* or red bean paste *(tau sa pow)*, tiny dumplings filled with pork *(siew mai)* and

Fresh produce for the kitchen

pork ribs steamed with black beans *(pai kwat)* are most commonly found in coffee shops.

Kway teow: flat, wide rice-flour noodles either fried *(goreng)* or dunked in a soup.

Laksa: a spicy Malay soup, usually enriched with coconut milk and chock full of prawns, chicken, noodles and beansprouts.

Mee: wheat-flour noodles served in a variety of ways; often fried with pork, prawns and vegetables or served in a soup.

Mee hoon (also *bee hoon*): dried rice-flour vermicelli, served the same way as *mee*.

Nasi campur: a Malay dish pronounced '*champur*', this is steamed rice accompanied by vegetable, chicken, seafood or beef dishes which the diner chooses from trays of cooked food on display.

Nasi goreng: the ubiquitous fried rice, with shrimp, beef or chicken.

Nasi padang: West Sumatran style of cooking, often toned down in Sabah but normally redolent with spices and chillies; the coconut beef *(rendang)*, curried fish *(otak)* and mild coconut-milk chicken *(opor ayam)* are some of the most popular dishes eaten with rice.

Ngau chap: a Chinese noodle soup with pieces of beef and tendon.

Roti canai: a light, flaky Indian bread fried on a griddle and served with lentils *(dhal)* or curry gravy. Excellent for breakfast.

Satay: Malaysian favourite of seasoned skewered beef, chicken or mutton grilled over charcoal and served with a spicy peanut sauce.

Soto: Malay/Javanese soup made with spices, chicken, beansprouts, potato and steamed rice cake.

Tom yam noodles: based on the favourite Thai soup filled with lemon, chillies and prawns, the local version adds lots of coconut milk and your choice of noodles, but do watch out for the spice!

A Kadazandusun speciality called hinava

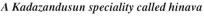

65

Local Fruits

Apart from offering the more common tropical fruits such as mango, papaya, pineapple and banana, Sabah has a great many unique fruits that will send fruit lovers into fibre nirvana. At one official party, a total of 43 wild fruits were served for a group of fruit enthusiasts from overseas. Some 15 or so varieties of mango are found, as well as a red-fleshed (usually a creamy yellow) durian and other strange delights. In the markets, some of the less common fruits you are likely to come across include the following:

Chiku: the South American sapodilla, this is a pale brown egg-shaped fruit that should be eaten when just starting to soften; it tastes like pears flavoured with maple syrup.

Durian: notorious for its pungent smell, this strange fruit looks like a spiky football. Inside are segments of buttery flesh which taste either like heaven or hell, depending on your personal reaction. Worth trying at least once. Look for durians just outside the entrance to Poring Hot Springs in the Kinabalu National Park; the trees there provides some superb fruit during the season, usually August/September. The unique red durians can be found at the Season Beaufort market.

Langsat: also known by their Filipino name, lanzones, they're small beige-coloured fruits enclosing segments of very sweet, juicy white flesh enclosing non-edible seeds.

Mangosteen: purplish black skin (that stains permanently, so be careful) with remarkably flavoured sweet-sour juicy segments with a non-edible seed.

Pomelo: giant yellow citrus fruit with very thick skin; either yellow or pink-fleshed inside, often very sweet and juicy.

Rambutan: hairy red exterior, succulent sweet white flesh and non-edible seed inside.

Starfruit: a yellow fruit with five-ridges, rather like a torpedo; sweet yet faintly astringent, juicy and very refreshing.

Soursop: irregular-shaped fruit, cut into slices. Mottled green exterior, and white fibrous flesh with a heavenly sweet-sour taste.

Sabah's unique red-fleshed durian

Sabah Specials

While you're here, don't miss the chance to sample a few of Sabah's unique vegetables. *Sayur manis* (also known as Sabah *choy*, Sabah vegetable or Sabah asparagus) is a local vegetable that has been developed to produce slender, crunchy stems with tender leaves at the top. Stir fried with *sambal belacan* (a spicy chilli paste) or dried prawns, or simply bathed with oyster sauce, the vegetable has a texture vaguely reminiscent of just-cooked asparagus but a flavour all its own. Take a leaf out of the jungle dweller's book and try young fern tips *(pakis)*, cooked the same way as *sayur manis*; very good to eat and full of vitamins too. Although *shiitake* mushrooms are not indigenous, they grow well on the slopes of the Crocker Range close to Kota Kinabalu. They are often referred to as Sabah mushrooms and are served in most Chinese restaurants, usually braised with oyster sauce.

Drinks

The usual canned and packaged drinks and, unless it is a Muslim establishment, beer and stout are available at coffee shops and restaurants throughout Sabah. Wine is available only at a few Western restaurants and major hotels. Fresh fruit juices squeezed from a range of fruits like avocado, starfruit, papaya, orange, banana and watermelon and the juice of young green coconuts are popular, as are a host of other local thirst quenchers like *cendol* (a combination of coconut milk, palm sugar syrup and bright green jelly-like strips made of mung bean flour), *leong foon* (squares of black seaweed jelly served with coconut milk and sugar syrup), *limau kasturi* (the juice of fresh small limes served with sour dried Chinese plums), soya bean milk, *tapai* (local rice wine found only at markets and at Kadazandusun and Murut celebrations; similar to Japanese sake).

Where to Eat

The ubiquitous *kedai kopi* or coffee shop is a Malaysian institution found all over Sabah, offering not only hot and cold drinks but food, often prepared by stall holders who sub-let from the owner. Food here is often very good and inexpensive. Don't ignore the rickety foodstalls either; you can often tell by the BMWs and expensive 4-wheel drives parked alongside that even the wealthiest gourmets don't turn their noses up at the surroundings if the food is good.

Many restaurants are simple, open-fronted shophouses, cooled by ceiling fans and usually very moderately priced. They rarely have menus and diners simply look at what's fresh for the day in the kitchen and make their requests accordingly. The cook or owner is invariably happy to make suggestions. Air-conditioned restaurants serving Chinese, Malay, Indian and other Asian cuisines, or various Western cuisines are found in the major towns and hotels.

Array of local fruit

Local hawker fare served in comfortable surroundings and Western fastfood such as fried chicken and pizzas can be found in air-conditioned shopping complexes such as Centrepoint and Wisma Merdeka.

Eating places outside of Kota Kinabalu are recommended in the various itineraries. On the following pages are places you might like to try while in Kota Kinabalu. Prices for a meal for two persons (excluding drinks) are categorised as follows:

$ = RM15
$$ = RM15–50
$$$ = over RM50

Asian Seafood

BEACH SEAFOOD RESTAURANT
Jalan Aru
Tanjung Aru Beach
Very casual open-air restaurant right near the beach, open every evening from 6pm. Good selection of fresh seafood, local vegetables and noodles. Beer available. $$

CHUAN HIN
Jalan Kolam
(next to Cottage Pub), Luyang
Tel: 235960
Very good, inexpensive barbecued seafood (especially ray and squid), *woh teh* dumplings and fried *kway teow*. A casual open-fronted establishment about 10 minutes from downtown Kota Kinabalu. Barbecued food served nightly from 6pm to midnight. $$

PORT VIEW SEAFOOD RESTAURANT
Jalan Haji Saman
(opposite the Marine Police)
Tel: 221753
Extremely popular with North Asian tour groups, this restaurant serves seafood from 6pm to 2am daily. Both the steamed live fish and prawns are incomparably sweet and well worth the high prices. Most dishes are prepared Chinese style. $$–$$$

Chinese

NAN XING HOTEL & RESTAURANT
Jalan Pantai
Tel: 212900/212399
Popular for *dim sum* in the mornings and for traditional Cantonese cuisine served in cool comfortable surroundings. Located in downtown Kota Kinabalu. $$

SHANG PALACE
Shangri-la's Tanjung Aru Resort
Tel: 225800
Elegant restaurant serving Cantonese

dishes for lunch and dinner, excellent *dim sum*. $$$

SEDCO SQUARE
Kampung Air
This casual open square, located between Centrepoint shopping complex and the BFO and Poring cinemas, is transformed into an outdoor eatery at around 6pm daily. The restaurants offer an array of seafood, meat and vegetables which they will prepare to order, while the stalls offer satay, noodles and other hawker fare. Sabah's best pan-fried 'pot-sticker' dumplings, or *woh teh*, as they're known here, are sold by a stall at one edge of the square. $–$$

SRI KAPITOL
1st floor, Hotel Capital
23 Jalan Haji Saman
(opposite Wisma Merdeka)
Tel: 231999
A true Malaysian restaurant, with a predominance of Chinese dishes (many with a local touch) as well as Malay favourites such as *ikan asam pedas* (sour fish curry) and *rendang* (spicy coconut beef). Usually packed at lunch time, partly due to its convenient downtown location and quality of food. $$

THE CHINESE RESTAURANT
Hyatt Kinabalu Hotel
Tel: 221234
Stylish modern restaurant with a good range of Cantonese cuisine. $$$

East-West
WISHBONE CAFE
Hotel Jesselton
69 Gaya Street
Tel: 223333
Pleasant, comfortable air-conditioned cafe popular at lunch time for its varied menu of favourite Chinese and Malay dishes. The Hainanese chicken rice – a simple dish of boiled chicken and rice served with a chilli-garlic sauce that tastes much better than it sounds – is especially good, plus a few Western items. Located near the banks and Sabah Tourism Promotion Council. $$

Malay
SRI RAHMAT
Ruang Tiong Hwa
Segama Complex
Right in the centre of Segama complex in downtown Kota Kinabalu, this is a good place for lunch, with an air-conditioned dining section. *Nasi campur*, rice served with ready-cooked dishes of your choice, is very good here. Open until 9pm daily. $

MELATI FOOD COURT
Basement Centrepoint Complex
(next to Pizza Hut)
A wide selection of tasty Malay and Indonesian favourites from 9.30am to 10pm daily. Try the tasty local 'salads' such as *rujak* and *gado-gado*, both tossed in a spicy peanut sauce. Also worthwhile is the *nasi campur* (steamed rice and a selection of meat, seafood and vegetable dishes). $

Indian
JOTHY'S RESTAURANT
Block 1, Lot 9, Api Api Centre
(not far from McDonalds, facing Coastal Highway)
The southern Indian food here, both vegetarian as well as meat, poultry and fish curries, is much the same as elsewhere in town, i.e. deliciously spicy, but the advantage of this restaurant is that it's air-conditioned and spotlessly clean. $

RESTORAN BILAL
Ruang Antarabangsa
Segama Complex
Good flaky Indian bread *(roti canai)*

and richly flavoured curries to go with it; the chicken liver curry is particularly good. Casual open-fronted restaurant right in centre of Kota Kinabalu and very popular with the locals. Open daily until 8pm. $

Thai

TAM NAK THAI
Block 5, 5G, Api Api Centre
Tel: 257328
A wide range of Thai favourites, well prepared and served in attractive surroundings by particularly helpful staff. There is a room available for private dining. $$$

Japanese

AZUMA
Wisma Merdeka
Jalan Tun Razak
Tel: 225533
The best Japanese food in town served in traditional surroundings. The usual *sushi* bar and a menu of popular Japanese dishes. Authentic food at the higher prices one always expects to pay for Japanese cuisine. $$$

NAGISA JAPANESE RESTAURANT
Hyatt Kinabalu Hotel
Tel: 221234
This stylish place, with huge windows overlooking the bay of Kota Kinabalu, is regarded as the best Japanese restaurant in town. Apart from the large dining room, there is a *sushi* counter and *tatami* room for traditional dining. Regular monthly promotions for lunch make this very popular with local businessmen and others who enjoy good Japanese cuisine. $$$

NISHIKI JAPANESE RESTAURANT
corner Gaya Street & Jalan Sengunting
Tel: 230582
Conveniently located opposite Sabah Tourism, this small restaurant offers Japanese food at modest prices. Their set lunches are good value. $$

Western

GARDENIA RESTAURANT
The Jesselton Hotel, 69 Gaya Street
Tel: 223333
The Gardenia is English in style with dark panelling and discreet lighting, and the mood intimate in the evenings. Right in the heart of downtown, the restaurant is popular for its moderately priced set lunch, with a choice of main courses. Have a drink and place your order from the adjacent Mountbatten Lounge, then when your meal is ready, adjourn to the restaurant to feast on US prime rib, oysters, lobsters and other delights. Wine is available by the glass or the bottle. $$$

LITTLE ITALY
Block 3, shop 33
Damai Plaza, Luyang
Tel: 251261
Run by charming Italian-Australian, Emiliano, this very popular restaurant makes its own delicious pastas and pizzas, and offers several other simple Italian dishes. It's only a short taxi ride from town, and well worth the trip. Closed Mondays. $$

PEPINOS
Shangri-La's Tanjung Aru Resort
Tel: 225800
Spacious restaurant with large terrace ideal for dining on balmy tropical evenings. Pepinos is dedicated to tried-and-true Italian favourites, with the emphasis on pastas and pizzas. The menu changes every three months; almost all the dishes on the specialities list are worth trying. Wine available by the glass. The prices are high by local standards, but the service and food are a cut above anything else in town. $$$

Fish drying in the tropical sun

Nightlife

To most people who live in Sabah, nightlife means sitting around over a good meal, having an outdoor barbecue and maybe nursing a drink or two with family or friends – if you're looking for wild, raunchy times, you've come to the wrong place in Asia. This is not to say you can't have fun, especially in Kota Kinabalu and some of the other big towns like Sandakan and Tawau.

Karaoke is a popular form of entertainment, as are discos, bars and music lounges, many with a section reserved for die-hard karaoke fans. For visitors looking for something different, a cultural show is performed at 8pm every Sunday evening at Shangrila's Tanjung Aru Resort. Enjoy a meal al fresco at Pulau Bayu Restaurant while watching local dance and music. Reservations are advised, and especially on weekends. Current night time hangouts in Kota Kinabalu include the following:

THE COTTAGE
Jalan Kolam
A popular pub. Friendly atmosphere, with a band playing nightly. German food served upstairs.

SEDCO SQUARE
Kampung Air
An open-air square where food stalls spring up every evening. A pleasant place to sit with a cold beer and watch the world go by.

SHENANIGANS
Hyatt Kinabalu Hotel
One of the most popular bars in town with good ambience, plenty of private corners and live music. Expect up-market prices.

SOMETHING AL'S
Shangri-La's Tanjung Aru Resort
The town's most sophisticated place to relax, with sound levels that encourage conversation. Play pool, board games, dance, or just have a drink – the choice is yours.

KK'S ENTERTAINMENT CLUB
The Pan Pacific Sutera
Relaxed and fun, KK's has live bands and great music spun by a DJ. Enjoy imported cigars, exotic cocktails and a range of creative pizzas.

Sports

With its superb beaches and clear waters, mountains, forests and rivers, Sabah offers the active and adventurous tourist plenty of sporting opportunities. You can tee off at a golf course carved from the forest almost 2,000m (6,562ft) up a mountain, scuba dive in the waters surrounding one of the world's most remarkable oceanic islands, shoot the rapids in a raging river, horse ride along a beach and around the rural countryside, speed over the waves in a catamaran or play tennis in the cool hours of dusk.

Scuba Diving

Sabah offers two world-class dive sites – Pulau Sipadan, an oceanic island off the southeast coast in the Celebes Sea, and Layang Layang, a remote atoll 300km (187 miles) from Kota Kinabalu in the South China Sea. There are also other dive sites near Sandakan and Semporna; locations nearby Kota Kinabalu are good for snorkeling and scuba training. Major dive operators in Sabah include the following:

Coral reefs bathed by translucent water make for excellent diving

Diving opportunities abound at the oceanic Sipadan island

BORNEO DIVERS & SEA SPORTS
9th floor, Menara Jubilee
53 Jalan Gaya
88000 Kota Kinabalu
Tel: 088-222226 Fax: 088-221500
Email: bdivers@po.jaring.my
The first and biggest diver operator in Sabah, and pioneer at the world-famous Pulau Sipadan; they run a first-class operation including diver training in Kota Kinabalu.

LAYANG LAYANG ISLAND RESORT
Unit A-9-3 Megan Phileo Avenue
12 Jalan Yap Kwan Seng
50450 Kuala Lumpur
Tel: 03-2622877 Fax: 03-2622980
Email: layang@pop.jaring.my
Operators of the luxurious dive resort of Layang Layang, an atoll in the South China Sea accessed by air from Kota Kinabalu. Their accommodation, food and diving are all first class.

PULAU SIPADAN RESORTS & TOUR
484 Bandar Sabindo
91021 Tawau
Tel: 089-765200 Fax: 089-763575
Email: psrt@po.jaring.my
They have two exclusive dive resorts, Kapalai near Sipadan, and Lankayan north of Sandakan, as well as a dive lodge on Pulau Sipadan.

SIPADAN DIVE CENTRE
A 10-04, Wisma Merdeka

88000 Kota Kinabalu
Tel: 088-240584 Fax: 088-240415
This company was one of the early operators on Pulau Sipadan, where it still maintains a dive lodge. Apart from a wildlife lodge at Sukau, they also have a resort on Pulau Tiga, which achieved fame as the location for the American TV series, *Survivor*.

SIPADAN WATER VILLAGE RESORT
Lot 3, 1st floor, Wisma MAA
Town Extension 11
91000 Tawau
Tel: 089-752996 Fax: 089-752997
Email: swvill@tm.net.my
Operators of a luxurious dive resort with chalets perched on the reef off Mabul island, near Pulau Sipadan.

White-Water Rafting

Sabah's best rivers for rafting are within easy reach of Kota Kinabalu, and range from a gentle float through rural scenery to adrenalin-pumping fights across tumultuous rapids. Most tour companies offer rafting packages.

Golf

Among the best courses in Sabah are the long-established 18-hole Sabah Golf and Country Club (tel: 088-224788) in Kota Kinabalu; the high-altitude 18-hole Kinabalu Golf Club (tel: 011-817396) on the slopes of Mount Kinabalu and the two Nicklaus-designed 18-hole courses at Borneo Golf Resort in Bongawan, an hour south of Kota Kinabalu (tel: 088-232350). The Sutera Harbour Golf and Country Club has a 27-hole championship course right on the edge of town (tel: 088-253131). Shangri-la's Rasa Ria Resort (tel: 088-225800) and Nexus Resort (tel: 088-411222/411030), both have good courses.

Mountain Biking

There are some lovely rides through rural areas around Kota Kinabalu, although enthusiasts claim the best trip is to cycle from Kinabalu Park Headquarters to Tamparuli. Contact Diethelm Borneo Expeditions at tel: 088-266353.

Horse Riding

There are several opportunities for days out on horseback in Sabah: gallop along the beach at sunrise, take a trail ride past the fields and villages as you explore rural life, or ride at low tide across to a nearby island. The Kindawan Riding Centre at Kinarut, 20 minutes from Kota Kinabalu, has horses to suit riders of varying ability, including ponies for children. If you wish, owner Dale Sinidol (tel: 088-225525) will fetch you from your hotel at no extra charge.

Calendar of Special Events

Thanks to its ethnic and religious diversity, Sabah celebrates a variety of traditional festivals, together with a number of unique sporting events. For the latest information on dates and special events, contact the Sabah Tourism Promotion Corporation (STPC). Also try the privately run Monsopiad Cultural Village, tel: 088-761366, which sometimes holds genuine Kadazandusun ceremonies offering a rare glimpse of these disappearing traditions.

January – March

Chinese New Year: Celebrated either in January or February, depending on the lunar calendar. The Lunar New Year is enthusiastically celebrated by Sabah's large Chinese community, with businesses and shops all over the state closing for their annual holiday.

A family reunion dinner on the eve of the New Year kickstarts the celebrations, which take place over the next 15 days. Lion dances are performed, drinking, feasting and merrymaking take place in homes, and little red packets with money are given to children and the unmarried.

Regatta Lepa Lepa (March): Traditional Bajau sailing boats take part in a colourful regatta off Semporna, the gateway to Pulau Sipadan.

Sabahans in traditional costume at a Harvest Festival celebration

Bajau horsemen in their festival finery

April – May

Pesta Ka'amatan (Harvest Festival) (May): Throughout the month of May, Kadazandusun tribes celebrate the successful harvesting of rice in villages all over the state, with ritual thanksgivings and a range of activities which culminate in the crowning of the Harvest Festival Queen (Unduk Ngadau). The festival is celebrated in Kota Kinabalu on 30 and 31 May at the Kadazandusun Cultural Association's headquarters, with cultural displays, traditional sports, handicraft demonstrations and the choosing of the Harvest Queen. Dates of the Harvest Festival celebrations in other locations can be obtained from the STPC.

Sabah Fest (May): Organised partly to give visitors an idea of the rich and diversified cultural heritage of Sabah, this includes a programme of cultural performances, cottage industries (weaving, basket making, beading and carving), a food fair and beach carnival. Lots of fun (and photographic opportunities) for everybody.

Vesak Day (May): Buddhists celebrate the birth, death and final enlightenment of Buddha with special prayers at temples, including the ritual washing of a Buddha image and circumambulation of stupas. The Goddess of Mercy (Kuan Yin) temple on Tuaran Road just before Inanam in Kota Kinabalu, and the big Pui Gin Tsen Buddhist temple on a hilltop on the outskirts of Sandakan, are good places to go on the morning of Vesak Day.

June – August

Dragon Boat Race (June): International and local dragon boats – long wooden canoes manned by a crew of around 20 – fighting it out in the waters of Likas Bay near Kota Kinabalu town.

Birthday of the Yang di-Pertuan Agung (5 June): A national festival honouring the supreme ruler (king)

Chinese New Year celebrations

of Malaysia, celebrated with parades on Kota Kinabalu's Padang.

National Day (31 August): Celebration of Malaysia's independence with parades and traditional dances.

October

Mount Kinabalu International Climathon: Held at Kinabalu Park, with climbers from many countries racing to the summit and back. Normally a 10-hour trip for lesser mortals (who break their climb on the first day to sleep overnight on the mountain), the record is 2 hours and 47 minutes, set in 1990.

Variable

Hari Raya Puasa: The date of this festival advances by roughly a month each year. Hari Raya Puasa is a Muslim celebration to mark the end of the *Ramadan*, the month during which Muslims are required to fast daily from sunrise to sunset. The day begins with prayers of thanksgiving in mosques all over Sabah, followed by a round of feasting and visiting. Delicious cakes are a hallmark of the festival, and with typical generosity, Sabah's Muslims will often invite foreign visitors into their home to share the celebrations. Hari Raya is an excellent opportunity to photograph Muslims in their finery.

On-Going Events

Tamu: Once an occasion for often mutually hostile tribes to meet and barter their goods in peace, the weekly markets or *tamu* are still popular in Sabah. Traders and buyers come from far and wide to buy and sell a fascinating array of goods from buffaloes to betel nuts, and catch up on gossip while downing glasses of rice wine *(tapai)*. Most interesting markets include Kota Belud and Tuaran (each Sunday), the Wednesday *tamu* at Tamparuli, and the Nabalu *tamu* each Thursday.

Gaya Street Fair: Kota Kinabalu's version of the *tamu*, when four blocks of Gaya Street are turned into an open-air market. The fair starts at around 7am every Sunday and runs until noon. There's everything from fruit to live puppies, tasty snacks to potted plants, local handicrafts to 'antiques'. Go early for the best bargains and to avoid the late-morning heat.

Dragon boat races are held in May

PRACTICAL information

GETTING THERE

By Air

Kota Kinabalu is connected by air with a number of regional capitals. The national carrier, MAS, operates daily flights from Kuala Lumpur in Peninsular Malaysia, and less frequent flights from Johor Bahru (Peninsular Malaysia), Singapore, Hong Kong, Taipei, Tokyo, Manila and Seoul. Kota Kinabalu is also serviced by flights from East Malaysia's Sarawak and the island of Labuan. A weekly flight connects Tawau (on the east coast of Sabah) with Tarakan in Kalimantan and Indonesia. Dragonair flies in from Hong Kong, while Singapore Airlines has twice weekly flights from Singapore. Indonesia's Merpati Airlines flies twice weekly from Tawau to Balikpapan, Kalimantan; Philippine Airlines has direct flights from Manila, while Royal Brunei flies between Bandar Seri Begawan in Brunei and Kota Kinabalu.

From the airport: As there is no direct bus service between Kota Kinabalu airport and the city, located just 7km (4 miles) away, visitors are advised to use a taxi if they are not met by a hotel or tour company bus. Fares to specific destinations should be paid for in advance at the taxi booking counter just outside the arrival halls, and the receipt given to the taxi driver. Locals usually choose to ignore this and pay the driver directly. Taxi charges range from about RM12–15, depending on your destination.

By Sea

Although cruise ships call in at Kota Kinabalu on occasion, there is no regular ship service to Sabah. There are at least three ferries per day between Kota Kinabalu and Labuan, with the possibility of onward connections to Brunei or Limbang, Sarawak. There is also a weekly ferry from Sandakan to Zamboanga, in the Philippines.

TRAVEL ESSENTIALS

When to Visit

Sabah enjoys a tropical climate, with temperatures ranging from 22°C to 30°C (72–86°F) in the lowland areas throughout the year. Although rain can occur at any time of year, showers are generally brief. During the northwest monsoon (November to April), strong winds and heavy rain can occur, especially December through February on the east coast. The southwest monsoon, especially during the months of July to September, brings rain to the west coast. Although

March–May is the best time to visit Saba

there is no well defined tourist season, the best months to visit are between March and May; March is the most reliable month for climbing Mount Kinabalu, while May, when the state celebrates the Harvest Festival, is particularly colourful. July and August are normally very busy months, making it strongly advisable to book accommodations in Kota Kinabalu and at Kinabalu Park well in advance.

Visas & Passports

Valid passports are required for entry into Sabah. Like neighbouring Sarawak, Sabah has its own immigration control so even if you are coming from Peninsular Malaysia, you will be required to go through immigration and customs on arrival in Kota Kinabalu. Your passport must be valid for at least 6 months from the time of your visit to Sabah.

Visas given on arrival are normally for 30 days, and can be extended for another 60 days at the Immigration Department in Kota Kinabalu.

Only citizens of Commonwealth countries, ASEAN, Ireland, Switzerland, the Netherlands and Lichtenstein do not need a visa to enter Sabah. Nationals of the following countries are also exempted from a visa for a visit not exceeding 3 months: Austria, Australia, Belgium, Denmark, Finland, France, Germany, Iceland, Italy, Japan, Luxembourg, Norway, South Korea, Sweden, Tunisia and USA. Citizens of Bulgaria, Rumania, Russia (CIS) and Yugoslavia are allowed a 7-day visa-free visit.

As visa requirements change from time to time, check with the relevant Malaysian embassy/consulate before leaving your home country.

Customs

There is no duty-free allowance for visitors arriving from Peninsular Malaysia or Sarawak. Those arriving from other destinations may bring in 250g of tobacco or cigars, or 200 cigarettes, plus a one-quart bottle of liquor.

Pornography, weapons and walkie-talkies are prohibited, while the possession of narcotics and other illegal drugs carries the death sentence. Firearms are subject to licensing.

Vaccinations

Sabah enjoys a high standard of health and vaccinations are not necessary. Visitors are required to produce a certificate of vaccination against yellow fever if they are travelling from an infected area.

Clothing

Comfortable, cotton clothing is ideal for Sabah's tropical climate. Although dress is less conservative than in Peninsular Malaysia, women will feel more comfortable if they do not wear extremely short skirts or shorts, or tight, revealing clothing. For most situations, shorts or a skirt with tee-shirts or cotton shirts are ideal. A sun hat (which can be bought locally) and sunglasses are strongly recommended. If you are planning on climbing Mount Kinabalu, be sure to bring warm clothing, including an anorak, hat and gloves, as the temperature on the summit can drop below zero. A light raincoat or poncho may also be useful.

If you're planning to go trekking in the rainforests, many experienced local 'jungle bashers' will tell you that shorts and tee-shirts are fine. Unless you are venturing through uncharted regions, it is not really necessary to wear trousers and long-sleeved shirts, which will make you a lot hotter in the humid forest. Good trainers are preferable to heavy leather boots, as there is often a problem keeping these dry. Leech socks (obtainable on

Wear the right clothes to trek

the 1st floor of Sandakan Market and from the Borneo Rainforest Lodge in Danum Valley Conservation Area) are recommended. The green-label Baygon insect repellent spray is the only one available in Sabah that is effective against leeches; spray around the ankles and feet, waist, neck and armpits. A light hat is also recommended. Be sure to bring a good pair of light binoculars, as well as a torch.

Electricity

Power is rated at 220 volts, 50 cycles. Electricity is available in all major towns and at most accommodation operated by Sabah Parks. A torch is recommended for travel to remote areas, and for use in the event of power failures.

Time Differences

Sabah time is 8 hours ahead of GMT, and 13 hours ahead of EST.

GETTING ACQUAINTED

Geography

Located between 5 and 7 degrees north of the equator, Sabah has been long been known as the 'Land Below the Wind', as it escapes the typhoons that slash a destructive path through the nearby Philippines. Occupying the northern tip of Borneo, the world's third largest island, Sabah is one of the 13 states of the Federation of Malaysia. It shares borders with Malaysian Sarawak to the southwest, and Indonesian Kalimantan to the south and southeast. Sabah's 1,400km (870 miles) of deeply indented coastline are washed by the waters of the South China Sea to the west, the Sulu Sea to the north and northeast, and the Celebes Sea to the east. Beautiful, unspoiled beaches abound, especially off the west coast, as well as on dozens of coral-fringed islands surrounding Sabah.

Most of Sabah is mountainous, with agriculture being carried out along the coastal plains and in occasional river valleys in the interior. The Crocker Range, which divides the west coast from the interior, culminates in the granite massif of Mount Kinabalu, at 4,093m (13,428ft), the tallest mountain between Irian Jaya

and the Himalayas. Dense forest – either lowland or montane rainforest or mangrove and riverine swamp forest – covers much of Sabah, making travel to remote regions often challenging.

Climate

Lowland areas of Sabah enjoy a pleasant tropical climate with the average daily temperature ranging from 22°C to 30°C (72–86°F). Relative humidity is quite high, but cooling breezes along the coast make for comfortable temperatures except during the hottest hours of early afternoon. At Kinabalu Park Headquarters (1,558m/5,111ft), the temperature generally is between 15–22°C (59–72°F), although at higher altitudes it can drop below zero. There are no strongly marked seasons in terms of temperature. The northeast monsoon, which blows from November to April, brings more rain and stronger winds than usual (especially to the east

A stick insect

coast). During the southwest monsoon (May to October), the west coast is more likely to receive rain, generally in the form of short, sudden squalls followed by clear skies.

Culture and Customs

Sabahans are particularly warm and friendly, and treat tourists with genuine kindness and courtesy. With more than 30 different ethnic groups living side by side in the state, locals have learned to be particularly tolerant of any unwitting breaches of etiquette.

A few tips worth remembering. It is customary to remove your shoes before entering a Muslim household (and most other homes too, for reasons of cleanliness). It is also considered rude to point at anything with the forefinger; use your entire hand to indicate a direction.

Muslims regard it as impolite to give or receive anything with the left hand, or to use the left hand when eating without a spoon and fork. Since you will not always be sure of a person's religion, it is safer to avoid using the left hand altogether in such circumstances.

Safety Precautions

As with any other city, it is wise to take precautions against petty theft in Kota Kinabalu, especially in the Central Market and Filipino Market.

MONEY MATTERS

Currency

The Malaysian currency is the Malaysian dollar or ringgit (abbreviated to RM), which is divided into 100 cents *(sen)*. Bank notes come in several denominations: RM2 (purple), RM5 (green), RM10 (red), RM 20 (brownish-orange), RM50 (bluish-green), RM100 (purple), RM500 (orange), and RM1,000 (dark green). Coins are worth either 5, 10, 20 and 50 sen, and RM1. RM1 bank notes are less frequently seen these days as they are currently being replaced by RM1 coins. You are permitted to bring in or take out unlimited amounts of Malaysian currency. Exchange rates fluctuate with the exception of US$, which is pegged at US$1 = RM3.80.

Credit Cards

Major credit cards such as American Express, Diners Club, MasterCard and Visa are accepted at the large hotels in Kota Kinabalu and other towns such as Sandakan, Tawau and Lahad Datu, as well as at a few restaurants in these locations. Cash, however, is a much safer bet in most circumstances (and is essential for bookings at Sabah Parks).

Money Changers

Money changers offer the best rate of exchange for cash and travellers' cheques, and queues are shorter than at banks. You are advised to change foreign currency in Kota Kinabalu before leaving for other areas in Sabah, where exchange rates may be less favourable and facilities limited.

Most registered money changers in Kota Kinabalu are located in Wisma Merdeka and Centrepoint.

One of Sabah's several pristine beaches

Tipping

A service charge of 10 percent and government tax of 5 percent is added to bills in tourist-class hotels and restaurants. More simple establishments do not impose any tax. Tipping is not normally the custom in Sabah; in many instances, it may even be refused.

Kinabalu, costs around RM100 for the entire taxi.

Buses

Buses leaving to a regular timetable provide inexpensive transport around the capital and to many other destinations in Sabah. Buses to Tanjung Aru Beach, (which pass by the State Museum), leave from the bus terminus opposite the Post Office near the Town Council (MPKK); look for a bus with the sign 'Tanjung Aru' together with either 'Beach' or 'Beach Hotel'; other buses simply marked 'Tanjung Aru' will stop at the village a good 10 minutes' walk from the beach.

Mini-buses, which leave from several locations around the town centre, provide fast, comfortable and moderately priced travel both within Kota Kinabalu and to most other major towns and even remote villages. Mini-buses to distant locations depart from in front of the town Padang (Green). These buses leave only when they have a full load of passengers, and charge from around RM5 a head (for Beaufort and Kota Belud), RM10 to Kinabalu Park Headquarters, RM20 for the 8-hour trip across to Sandakan; and RM50 to Tawau.

Mini-buses can also be hired for special trips, such as between Ranau and Poring Hot Springs at Park Headquarters, or chartered for the day. Prices can be negotiated from around RM200 for a full day with the driver.

Rail

Borneo's only rail service runs from Tanjung Aru station in Kota Kinabalu, via Beaufort to Tenom. The train is very slow, and most people prefer to travel to Beaufort by mini-bus. However, a ride through the Padas River Gorge to Tenom either by the small railcar (departing Beaufort at 8.20am weekdays only) or by regular train is well worthwhile. Book in advance by calling the Stationmaster at Beaufort tel: 087-211518. Train buffs can enjoy a ride in an old train, restored to colonial splendour, travelling between Tanjung Aru and Papar; food is served, with a tour of Papar included. Call 088-254611 for further information.

GETTING AROUND

Air

Kota Kinabalu and the major Sabah towns like Sandakan, Lahad Datu, Tawau and Kudat are connected by regular MAS services. Flights are often full, especially at weekends or during holidays, so book in advance. Fixed wing aircraft and helicopters can be chartered from Sabah Air in Kota Kinabalu.

Taxis

The majority of taxis in Sabah are air-conditioned and without meters. As drivers of the few taxis equipped with meters are reluctant to use them, you must establish the price first before commencing your journey. Taxis, which are generally painted white with the name of the operator on the front doors, can be hailed off the street or boarded from a taxi stand in major towns. Taxis in Kota Kinabalu can be called at tel: 088-253282. Be sure to have exact details of your destination as taxi drivers do not use street directories or maps and frequently have problems locating suburban destinations.

A popular way of travelling to destinations up to four hours or so away from the major towns is by 'outstation taxi'. These provide a comfortable, moderately priced, non-stop ride for up to 4 passengers; you can either share the taxi or rent it completely for the trip. For instance, the trip to Tenom, four hours from Kota

Car Rental

Although technically an International Driver's Licence should be shown for hiring a self-drive car in Sabah, most companies are happy to accept a valid licence from your country of residence. Hire prices range from RM140 per day for a self-drive sedan to a minimum of RM230 for a chauffeur-driven vehicle. Luxury models and 4-wheel drive vehicles cost from RM240 upwards.

Driving in Sabah is on the left-hand side of the road. Major roads are well signposted, but if you intend going off the beaten track, be sure you obtain a good map and explicit directions in advance. Hire cars can be booked at the airport on arrival, at your hotel or at rental companies in Kota Kinabalu town.

E & C Rent a Car
2nd floor, 258 Kompleks Karamunsing
Tel: 088-239996

Kinabalu Rent a Car
Lot 3, 61 3rd floor
Komplex Karamunsing
Tel: 088-232602/232603
The company also has branches at Hyatt Hotel, Shangri-la's Tanjung Aru Resort and Kota Kinabalu Airport.

Padas Jaya Rent a Car
G20, Ground Floor, Wisma Sabah
Tel: 088-233239/239936
They have a range of cars including Protons and larger Toyotas.

Ferry Services

Regular ferry services to the islands making up the Tunku Abdul Rahman Park, just off Kota Kinabalu, leave from the

Mini-bus to Beaufort

jetties in front of the Hyatt Kinabalu Hotel, and from the marina at Shangri-La's Tanjung Aru Resort. Boats leaving from the waterfront near the Hyatt Kinabalu charge around RM10 per person to Pulau Manukan, Pulau Mamutik and Pulau Sapi, RM12 to Pulau Sulug and RM20 to Police Beach on Pulau Gaya. All fares quoted are return. In addition, a regular service from Sabah Parks' jetty to Pulau Manukan leaves at 8.50am, 10am, noon and 4pm daily and the fare is RM10 per person return.

Air-conditioned ferries for Labuan leave daily from in front of the Hyatt with onward connections to Brunei and Lawas in Sarawak. It is generally best to book one day ahead if travelling on a weekend or public holiday.

Business Hours

Most food markets are in full swing by 7am, although shops and offices generally open around 8.30am or 9am, and close between 5pm and 6pm. Supermarkets and department stores are open 7 days a week, usually from 9am until 9pm.

Government offices (including Immigration) work the following hours:

Monday to Thursday: 8am–12.45pm and 2–4.30pm; Friday: 8am–11.30am and 2–4.30pm; Saturday: 8am–12.45pm.

Banks are open 10am–3pm Monday to Friday, and 9.30–11.30am on Saturday. Banks and all government offices (including Immigration Department and the Post Office) are closed on the first and third Saturday of each month.

Public Holidays

The following are official public holidays in Sabah. As dates of ethnic festivals are determined by the various lunar calendars, check first with the Sabah Tourism Promotion Corporation (STPC) office.

New Year's Day: 1 January
Chinese New Year: January/February
Hari Raya Puasa: Date varies
Good Friday: April
Labour Day: 1 May
Awal Muharram: Date varies

Picturesque Tanjung Aru Resort

Harvest Festival: 30/31 May
Vesak Day: May
HM the King's Birthday: 5 June
Hari Raya Haji: Date varies
National Day: 31 August
TYT's Birthday: 16 September
Prophet Muhammad's Birthday: Date varies
Deepavali: October/November
Christmas Day: 25 December

ACCOMMODATION

Top quality tourist hotels in Sabah are currently limited to Kota Kinabalu and nearby beach resorts, and Sandakan and Tawau. Other accommodation ranges from clean and comfortable to the basic. Sabah Parks offers a range of accommodation in Kinabalu Park, Pulau Manukan, Pulau Mamutik, Pulau Tiga and the 'turtle island' of Pulau Selingan.

The Malaysian government is encouraging home-stays, an interesting and inexpensive way to get to know the locals; check with STPC for the latest listings.

The following suggestions range from the least expensive single accommodation to the most luxurious double accommodation available. Unless specified, prices do not include the requisite 10 percent service charge and 5 percent government tax.

$	=	less than RM60 single
$$	=	RM60–150
$$$	=	over RM150

Kota Kinabalu

AZUMA
2nd Floor, Wisma Merdeka
Jalan Tun Razak
Tel: 088-225533
$$$

BACKPACKER LODGE
Lot 25 Lorong Dewan, Australia Place
Tel: 088-261495
Two dormitories and two double rooms. Simple accommodation with ceiling fans, common shower and TV in a quiet corner of town, right next to the old Police Station. $

BERJAYA PALACE HOTEL
1 Jalan Tanki Karamunsing

PO Box 10453, 88805 Kota Kinabalu
Tel: 088-211911
Fax: 088-211600
Tucked away on a quiet hill behind the Komplex Karamunsing, this hotel is only a RM5 taxi ride from the centre of town. Full room facilities, as well as restaurants, business centre, travel services and swimming pool. $$

CASUARINA HOTEL
Lg Ikan Lais, off Jalan Mat Salleh
Tanjung Aru
Tel: 088-243899
Fax: 088-223000
Attractive, small, well equipped hotel with bar and restaurant about 3 minutes' walk from Tanjung Aru beach. Very friendly service with free transport to the city and airport. Excellent choice unless you're looking for a swimming pool. $$

HOTEL HOLIDAY
1st floor, Block F
Segama Shoppping Complex
Tel: 088-213116
Fax: 088-215576
Clean and comfortable centrally located hotel with air-conditioned rooms and bathroom attached; mini-bar, TV and in-house video. $$

HOTEL JESSELTON
69 Gaya Street, PO Box 19401
88000 Kota Kinabalu
Tel: 088-223333
Fax: 088-240401
Kota Kinabalu's first hotel underwent a total transformation in the mid-1990s and has taken on a new lease of life as a charming 33-room boutique hotel in the heart of town. Offers the Mountbatten Lounge as well as a Western grill room and popular coffee house. $$$

HYATT KINABALU HOTEL
Jalan Datuk Salleh Sulong

Locked Bag 47, 88994 Kota Kinabalu
Tel: 088-219888
Fax: 088-225972
350 rooms and suites. Full room facilities, restaurants, swimming pool, business centre, health centre, travel services and shops (including the city's best bread, cakes and pizza in the delicatessen). $$$

THE MAGELLAN SUTERA
Sutera Habour Boulevard
Tel: 088-312222
Fax: 088-312020
With 456 rooms, four restaurants, Kota Kinabalu's largest ballroom and a huge freeform swimming pool, this hotel is the star of the Sutera Harbour complex. Guests may also use the restaurants of The Pacific Sutera, and the Sutera Harbour Golf and Country Club, plus its marina. $$$

THE PACIFIC SUTERA
Sutera Harbour Boulevard
Tel: 088-318888
Fax: 088-317777
One of the two hotels in the Sutera Harbour complex, which includes a marina, 27-hole golf course and sports facilities overlooking the islands of the Tunku Abdul Rahman Marine Park. $$$

PULAU MANUKAN CHALETS
20 two-bedroom chalets, allow 4 persons each. These chalets have an electric kettle

Superior room at Rasa Ria Resort

and fridge as well as air-conditioned bedrooms. There is a restaurant, swimming pool and squash court on Manukan which is part of Tunku Abdul Rahman Marine Park. Book at Kinabalu Nature Resorts, ground floor, Wisma Sabah, tel: 088-243629, 245742, fax: 088-242861. $$

SEASIDE TRAVELLERS INN
Km 20, Kota Kinabalu/Papar Highway
Kinarut
Tel: 088-750555
Fax: 088-223399
Small, family-run inn popular with families and travellers, located right on the waterfront at Kinarut Beach, just 20 minutes south of Kota Kinabalu. Dining room, TV room and barbecue area. $

SHANGRI-LA'S TANJUNG ARU RESORT
Locked Bag 174, 88999 Kota Kinabalu
Tel: 088-225800
Fax: 088-217155
500 rooms and suites. Arguably Kota Kinabalu's most luxurious hotel. Tennis, swimming pool, gymnasium, health centre, marina with sea sports and children's playground are currently offered, as well as a selection of bars, restaurants and a business centre. $$$

TREKKER'S LODGE
Jalan Pantai
Tel: 088-213888
Fax: 088-262818
Clean air-conditioned dormitories, a laundry and a wealth of travel information available in a good location. $

Pantai Dalit

SHANGRI-LA'S RASA RIA RESORT
Pantai Dalit, PO Box 600, 89208 Tuaran
Tel: 088-792888
Fax: 088-792000
Set in 160 hectares (400 acres) of land, this superbly located resort is fringed by a private beach and bounded by two rivers. The site also includes a forested headland occupied by a wildlife sanctuary plus an 18-hole golf course. Excellent range of recreational facilities, restaurant, coffee shop, lounge bar and supermarket. $$$

Karambunai

NEXUS GOLF RESORT KARAMBUNAI
Menggatal
Tel: 088-411222/411030
Fax: 088-411020/412028
Email: nexushtl@tm.net.my
This luxurious seaside resort, just 30 minutes by highway from the city, has excellent facilities and food, including the best

dim sim in Sabah in its Chinese restaurant. $$$

Kinabalu Park

Accommodation within Kinabalu Park was privatised in 1998, and must now be booked through Kinabalu Nature Resorts, ground floor, Wisma Sabah, Kota Kinabalu, tel: 088-243629, 245742, 246803; fax: 088-242861. Accommodation at **Park Headquarters** ranges from budget-priced hostels with dormitories and kitchen facilities, to twin-bed cabins ($$), and lodges with cooking facilities ($$$).

The Laban Rata Rest House ($$), Gunting Lagadan Hostel ($), Waras Hut ($) and Sayat Sayat Hut ($) are all en route for the summit.

At **Poring Hot Springs**, accommodation ranges from hostels with cooking facilities ($) to cabins ($$) and chalets ($$$). The relatively new **Mesilau Nature Resort** on the eastern side of Kinabalu Park has chalets and lodges ($$–$$$).

Kundasang

HOTEL PERKASA MT KINABALU
WDT 11, 89309 Ranau
Tel: 088-889511
74 rooms. Located about 5km (3 miles) from Kinabalu Park, this hotel sits on a hilltop looking over Kundasang area towards the summit of Mount Kinabalu. Full room facilities, restaurant, bar, tennis, shops. Within half-hour of the Mount Kinabalu golf course. $$

KINABALU PINE RESORT
Kundasang
Tel: 088-889388
Attractive well-equipped chalets in a pleasant setting facing Mount Kinabalu; probably the nicest accommodation outside the park. $$$

Sabah Parks' jetty

KINABALU ROSE COTTAGE
Km 18, Ranau Road
Tel: 088-889233
Somewhat flashy although far from luxurious, this 17-room hotel has good views and a restaurant, and is popular with Chinese families from Kota Kinabalu. About five minutes' drive from Kinabalu Park. $$

Sinsuron Pass

GUNONG EMAS MOTEL & RESTAURANT
Kilometre 52
Kota Kinabalu/Tambunan Road
Tel: 088-213116
Located at around 1,600m near Sinsuron Pass on the Crocker Range, an hour's drive from Kota Kinabalu, Gunong Emas offers a range of conventional rooms plus 20 'Tarzan and Jane' treehouses, built around living trees on a very steep hillside. The restaurant is extremely popular with travellers, while the small private zoo on the site also attracts visitors. $$

Lankayan Island

LANKAYAN DIVE RESORT
Langkayan Island
Tel: 089-765200
Fax: 089-763575/763563
Email: psrt@po.jaring.my
A luxurious dive resort on its own coral island in the Sulu Sea, north of Sandakan. Good wreck dives and corals nearby.

Sandakan

SANDAKAN RENAISSANCE HOTEL
Jalan Utara, Km 1
Tel: 089-213299
Fax: 089-271271
120 rooms and suites. The only 5-star hotel in Sandakan, this incorporates the old Sabah hotel built around the historic governor's house. Full room facilities, business centre, conference room and ballroom. $$$

SANBAY
Off Jalan Leila, 2km
Tel: 089-275000
Fax: 089-275575
Pleasant 65-room hotel with modern conveniences including a bar/restaurant. Just a short taxi ride from the town centre. $$

Idyllic Pulau Sipadan

Sepilok

SEPILOK NATURE RESORT
2.5km Sepilok Road
Tel: 089-535001
Fax: 089-535002
A luxurious resort adjacent to the Orangutan centre, in a garden setting. Timber air-conditioned chalets with private verandahs looking over the gardens. $$$

UNCLE TAN'S
Block B, Lot 8, SUDC Shops
Gum Gum, Mile 16
Tel: 089-531639
A long-time budget travellers' favourite, Uncle Tan still offers an incredible deal at RM20 for full board. His original house burned down and he is now located in a shophouse between Sepilok and Sandakan. Uncle Tan also offers wildlife tours on the Kinabatangan River. $

WILDLIFE LODGE
Sepilok Jungle Resort, Sepilok Road
Tel: 089-533031
Fax: 089-533029
Located just a few minute's walk from the orang-utan sanctuary, this resort sprawls over huge landscaped gardens. Very friendly owners and good food in the attractive open-sided restaurant. Accommodation from budget dormitory to air-conditioned rooms; free pick-up from the main road (use the phone in the nearby store); competitively priced day tours to Sukau. $–$$

Pulau Selingan

PULAU SELINGAN
9th Floor, Wisma Khoo Saik Chiew
Tel: 089-273453
Fax: 089-274718
Three chalets accommodating total of 20 people. Book in advance through Assistant Parks Warden *(see Itinerary 11)* for

accommodation in these chalets. Restaurant with basic food and drinks. $

Sukau, Kinabatangan River

Five tour operators have lodges along the Kinabatangan River, at Sukau: two at the end of the road and the remainder about 5 minutes upriver. Book in advance in Kota Kinabalu; the cost of accommodation, meals and guide is included in the tour price. Recommended lodges include:

PROBOSCIS LODGE
Sipadan Dive Centre
Tel: 088-240584
Fax: 088-240415
Beautiful private chalets in spacious garden; the most attractive accommodation of all, with good guides as well.

SUKAU RAINFOREST LODGE
Borneo Eco Tours
Tel: 089-220210
Fax: 089-213614
Popular place; rooms are small but there's a spacious communal sitting and dining area.

SUKAU RIVER LODGE
Wildlife Expeditions
Tel: 088-254300, 089-219616
Fax: 088-231758, 089-214570
Wildlife Expeditions pioneered tourism in the region and still offer a thoroughly professional service. Their accommodation is somewhat cramped, however.

Tenom

ANTANOM HOTEL
PO Box 78, 89908 Tenom
Tel: 087-736381
10 rooms. Located on the main street with clean, comfortable rooms, attached bathrooms and TV. Ask for a room away from the karaoke lounge. $

HOTEL PERKASA
PO Box 225, 89908, Tenom
Tel: 087-735811
63 rooms. Full room facilities plus restaurant, bar and conference rooms. Located on hill overlooking Tenom. Call the hotel from Tenom Station and they will pick you up. $$

Tawau

BELMONT MARCO POLO HOTEL
PO Box 1003, 91007 Tawau
Tel: 089-777988
150 rooms. Tawau's best hotel, with full room facilities, restaurants and a bar. $$

HOTEL ORIENTAL
10 Jalan Dunlop
Tel: 089-771500
29 rooms. Located in the centre of Tawau, air-conditioned rooms. $$

LOONG HOTEL
Jalan Wing Lok
Tel: 089-765305
Quiet, clean and comfortable accommodation. Good value for money.

Kudat

HOTEL KINABALU
1 Block C, Sedco Shophouse, Kudat
Tel: 088-613888
18 rooms. Air-conditioned rooms with TV, private bathroom. $

KAMPUNG BAVANGGAZO LONGHOUSE
via Jln Tinangol, Matunggong
21 twin rooms. Price includes dinner and breakfast. Book at the Sabah Tourism Promotion Corporation (STPC) at tel: 088-219400. See also *Itinerary 7.* $

Semporna

DRAGON INN
Semporna Ocean Tourism Centre
Tel: 089-781088
Fax: 089-781088
22 rooms. Built on stilts over the sea (which is not suitable for swimming) with a popular seafood restaurant. $$

Pulau Sipadan

The number of visitors staying at the simple but comfortable accommodation on

Kinabalu Park chalets

Pulau Sipadan, run by different dive operators, is now severely limited by the government; alternative accommodation is available on the nearby islands of Mabul and Kapalai. Dive operators on Sipadan include:

BORNEO DIVERS
Tel: 088-222226
Fax: 088-221550

PULAU SIPADAN RESORT
Tel: 089-765200
Fax: 089-763575

SIPADAN DIVE CENTRE
Tel: 088-240584
Fax: 088-240415

Pulau Mabul

SIPADAN MABUL RESORT
Tel: 088-230006
Beach-front with small swimming pool, modest chalets dotted about the grounds.

SIPADAN WATER VILLAGE RESORT
Tel: 089-752996
Fax: 089-752997
Luxurious wooden chalets built on stilts over the reef; this well-run beautiful resort is part-Japanese owned.

Pulau Kapalai

KAPALAI DIVE RESORT
Tel: 089-765200
Fax: 089-763575
Tiny exclusive dive resort on a reef between Mabul and Sipadan; run by Pulau Sipadan Resort and Tours, who also have dive operations at Lankayan and Sipadan.

Lahad Datu

THE EXECUTIVE HOTEL
Jalan Teratai
Tel: 089-881333
Fax: 089-881777
The newest and best hotel in town; the 50 attractive rooms are equipped with the latest facilities. There is also a lounge bar, coffee house and Chinese restaurant. $$

HOTEL OCEAN
1st floor, Jalan Cempaka
Tel: 089-881700

Budget hotel in the middle of one of the busy main streets in town; basic but clean and good value. $

Danum Valley

BORNEO RAINFOREST LODGE
Kota Kinabalu Office
PO Box 11622, 88817 Kota Kinabalu
Tel: 088-243245/244100
Fax: 088-244140/262050 or
Lahad Datu Office
Block 3, Ground floor
Fajar Centre (near airport)
Tel: 089-885051
Fax: 089-883091
An international-class jungle lodge set in the Danum Valley Conservation Area. Accommodation is in attractive wooden bungalows with bathroom and balcony. $$$

HEALTH AND EMERGENCIES

Hygiene/General Health

Sabah has a high standard of hygiene and visitors can safely eat and drink virtually anywhere. Naturally, if any establishment or food stall looks unsanitary, shun it as you would in your own country. Bottled water is available in supermarkets; if you ask for water in restaurants or coffee shops, it will have been boiled, and ice is safe.

If travelling to remote villages, it is advisable to take malaria prophylactics, starting your course before arrival in Sabah. Be sure to use sunscreen, especially when travelling along the coast, and drink more water than usual to avoid dehydration.

A mosquito repellent is often necessary, and when reinforced by a lighted mosquito coil (sold throughout Sabah), will ensure a good night's sleep in areas where mosquitoes may be a problem.

Pharmacies

Most medicines are widely available and dispensed by trained pharmacists in major towns. Even in remote areas, you will find the local Chinese 'medical hall' selling a supply of basic medicines. It is a good idea to travel with an antiseptic or even antibiotic cream such as Garamycin for use on any scratches or cuts, which can

easily become infected in Sabah's hot, humid climate. Chinese Po Chai pills, an effective local remedy for 'traveller's tummy', are widely available.

Clinics and Hospitals

Sabah enjoys a high standard of health care, with private clinics, government hospitals and polyclinics found even in remote areas.

Many doctors are Western-trained and speak English as do nursing staff. Government hospitals will accept foreign patients in any emergency. For non-emergency cases, go to the outpatient clinic for a consultation, although be prepared for a long wait. Your hotel will be able to advise you should you need a private medical practitioner.

The most highly regarded medical centre in the state, **Sabah Medical Centre**, tel: 088-424333, is located in Likas about 10 minutes north of the centre of Kota Kinabalu. Alternatively, go to the **Queen Elizabeth Hospital**, Kota Kinabalu, tel: 088-54911. In Sandakan, the **Duchess of Kent Hospital**, tel: 089-212111 is recommended, as is the **Tawau General Hospital** in Tawau, tel: 089-773533.

COMMUNICATION AND NEWS

Postal and Telecommunications Services

The mail service in Sabah is regretably not as efficient as it should be, and letters often taken longer to arrive than expected. Post offices are found in all towns; the General Post Office (Pejabat Pos Besar) at Jalan Tun Razak in Kota Kinabalu maintains a separate counter for Poste Restante. Buy stamps at counters marked 'Stem' and post your overseas letters in the post boxes marked 'Luar Negeri'.

The telecommunications system works well, with international direct dialing and operator-assisted calls available from major hotels (who normally impose a service charge) as well as from the Telekoms Office at Jalan Tunku Abdul Rahman in Kota Kinabalu. Large denomination phone cards for both Telekom and Uniphone telephones can be used for overseas calls in booths marked IDD; several are located outside the

General Post Office. Telegram, telefax and telex services are available at major hotels in Sabah, as well as Telekom offices in major towns.

To call Sabah from overseas, dial the international country code 60 for Malaysia, followed by respective area codes: 88 (Sabah and Kudat); 87 (Tenom); and 89 (Sandakan, Lahad Datu and Tawau).

Useful numbers in Kota Kinabalu include the following:
Police, tel: 212222
Hospital, tel: 218166
Trunk calls, tel: 101
Directory enquiry, tel: 103
International calls, tel: 108
AT&T, tel: 1-800-80-0011
MCI, tel: 1-800-80-0012
Sprint, tel: 1-800-80-0016

Media

There are three daily English-language newspapers – the *Borneo Mail*, *Sabah Times* and the *Daily Express* – which include local and overseas news, advertisements for films and a column of coming events ('What's On' and 'Sabah Week'). Peninsular Malaysia newspapers (the *New Straits Times* and the *Star*) are also widely available, while some hotels carry international newspapers.

Sabah has its own radio station, and also receives television programmes in Malay, Chinese and English from Peninsular Malaysia on Channels 1, 2 and 3. CNN is available via satellite TV (Astro).

LANGUAGE

The Malay language, or Bahasa Malaysia, is polysyllabic, with variations in syllables to convey changes in meaning, unlike tonal languages such as Mandarin, Cantonese and Thai. For example, *duduk* (sit) is a verb. By adding the prefix *ke* and suffix *an*, we get the noun *kedudukan*, which means position. By adding a different prefix, *pen*, we get another noun, *penduduk*, which means inhabitant. Adding an *i* after *duduk* turns it into an active verb (to sit), while *menduduki* is a present continuous verb.

Tones do not vary to give different meanings and, for the most part, words are pronounced as they are spelt. In general, the pronunciation is the same as in English, with a few exceptions.

In Bahasa Malaysia, 'a' is pronounced 'ar' as in tar. The letter 'e' has an 'er' sound, as in reserve. You will also find that 'c' is pronounced 'ch' as in chair; the letter 'g' is always hard, as in gun and garden, not as in ginger; and 'sy' is pronounced 'sh'.

The language uses two distinct scripts: *Jawi* and *Rumi*. Jawi is the Arabic form of writing; *Rumi* the Roman alphabet, considered the easier of the two and also the official script of the country.

Here is a small vocabulary to get you on your way.

Numbers

1	*Satu*
2	*Dua*
3	*Tiga*
4	*Empat*
5	*Lima*
6	*Enam*
7	*Tujuh*
8	*Lapan*
9	*Sembilan*
10	*Sepuluh*
11	*Sebelas*
12	*Dua belas*
13	*Tiga belas*
20	*Dua puluh*
21	*Dua puluh satu*
100	*Seratus*
200	*Dua ratus*
1,000	*Seribu*

Greetings and Others

How do you do?	*Apa khabar?*
Good morning	*Selamat pagi*

Panar Laban Guesthouse, Mount Kinabalu

Good afternoon	*Selamat petang*	How far?	*Berapa jauh?*
Good evening	*Selamat malam*	I want to go to...	*Saya hendak*
Goodbye	*Selamat tinggal*		*pergi ke...*
Bon voyage	*Selamat jalan*	Stop here	*Tolong berhenti*
Fine/good	*Baik*		*sini*
Thank you	*Terima kasih*	Expensive	*Mahal*
Please	*Tolong/sila*	Lower the price	*Kurang harganya*
Excuse me	*Maafkan saya*	Too big	*Besar sangat*
I am sorry	*Saya minta maaf*	Too small	*Kecil sangat*
Yes	*Ya*	Any other colour?	*Ada warna lain?*
No	*Tidak*		

Pronouns

I	*Saya*
You	*Anda/awak*
He/she	*Dia*
We	*Kami*
They	*Mereka*

Forms of Address

Mr	*Encik*
Mrs	*Puan*
Miss	*Cik*

Directions and Travel

Where	*Di mana*
Right	*Kanan*
Left	*Kiri*
Turn	*Belok*
Go	*Pergi*
Stop	*Berhenti*
Follow	*Ikut*
Near	*Dekat*
Far	*Jauh*
Inside	*Dalam*
Outside	*Luar*
Front	*Hadapan*
Behind	*Belakang*
Here	*Sini*
There	*Sana*
Road/street	*Jalan*
Bridge	*Jambatan*
Junction	*Simpang*
North	*Utara*
South	*Selatan*
East	*Timur*
West	*Barat*

Useful Phrases

How much?	*Berapa harganya?*
Can you help me?	*Bolehkah encik*
	tolong saya?
Where is this	*Di mana tempat*
place?	*ini?*

Other Handy Words

Drink	*Minum (verb),*
	Minuman (noun)
Eat	*Makan (verb),*
	Makanan (noun)
Fruit	*Buah-buahan*
Water	*Air*
Have	*Ada*
Don't have	*Tidak ada*
Toilet	*Tandas*
Why?	*Mengapa?*
When?	*Bila?*
Hot (spicy)	*Pedas*
Hot (heat)	*Panas*
Cold	*Sejuk*
Sweet	*Manis*
Sour	*Masam*
Delicious	*Sedap*
Clean	*Bersih*
Dirty	*Kotor*
Beautiful	*Cantik*
Open	*Buka*
Close	*Tutup*
Never	*Tidak pernah*
Often	*Selalu*
Sometimes	*Kadang-kadang*

USEFUL INFORMATION

Tourist Offices

Free brochures, advice, information on current events etc can be obtained at the **Sabah Tourism Promotion Corporation** (STPC). Located in a beautifully restored, white colonial building (one of only three to survive the bombing of World War II) in Gaya Street, Kota Kinabalu, the STPC can be contacted at tel: 088-219400.

Just around the corner from the STPC, on the ground floor of Eon CMG Life Building in Jalan Seguntung, is the office of the **Malaysian Tourism Promotion Board** (MTPB). Although it has some

Frolicking kids

brochures on Sabah, MTPB specialises in information on other regions of Malaysia (tel: 088-211732).

Photography

The hot, humid climate of Sabah makes it advisable to carry your camera in a closed bag with sachets of silica gel to absorb the moisture. Print film is widely available in Kota Kinabalu and other towns throughout the state.

Standard slide film such as Kodachrome and Fujichrome are available in Kota Kinabalu, but if you want to use high-speed slide film, it is advisable to bring it with you. Film processing for all but Kodachrome is available in major towns, including 1-hour processing of prints at the souvenir shop at Kinabalu Park.

Because of strong light in Sabah, you will obtain best results if you shoot before 10am and after 4pm, when colour density is better and side lighting gives you a more interesting picture. Most Sabahans are happy to have their photograph taken, but it is always polite to ask first.

For quick processing of print and slide films, as well as a range of film, cameras and accessories (plus professional advice if needed), go to Golden City Colour Centre Trading Co, Lot 7, Block C, Segama Shopping Complex or its branch at G22, Centrepoint.

USEFUL ADDRESSES

Banks

Sabah banks prefer US$ to any other currency. Some actually refuse to change any other currency. Some major banks are:

Kota Kinabalu

HONGKONG BANK
56 Jalan Gaya
Tel: 088-212622

MALAYAN BANKING BERHAD
Jalan Pantai
Tel: 088-219594

STANDARD CHARTERED BANK
20 Jalan Haji Saman
Tel: 088-238289

OVERSEA-CHINESE BANKING CORPORATION LTD
65 Jalan Gaya
Tel: 088-232494

Sandakan

HONGKONG BANK
Jalan Pelabuhan/Lebuh Tiga
Tel: 089-213122

STANDARD CHARTERED BANK
Jalan Pelabuhan
Tel: 089-275428

Tawau

HONGKONG BANK
210 Jalan North
Tel: 089-775869

STANDARD CHARTERED BANK
518 Jalan Habib Husin
Tel: 089-771745

Airline Offices

The following airline offices are all found in Kota Kinabalu.

DRAGONAIR
Ground floor, Kompleks Karamunsing
Tel: 088-254733

MALAYSIA AIRLINES
Ground floor, Kompleks Karamunsing
Tel: 088-213555

ROYAL BRUNEI
Ground floor, Kompleks Kuasa
Tel: 088-242193/242194

SINGAPORE AIRLINES
Ground floor, Kompleks Kuasa
Tel: 088-255449

Tour Operators

There are several competent tour operators offering trips to major places of interest. Here are some companies recommended for their special expertise in certain areas:

BORNEO ADVENTURE
10th floor, Wisma Gaya, Kota Kinabalu
Tel: 088-238731
Fax: 088-238730
Personalised service from thoroughly professional company with head office in Kuching, Sarawak.

DIETHELM BORNEO TOURS
303, 3rd floor, Eon CMG Life Building
Jalan Segunting, Kota Kinabalu
Tel: 088-222721
Fax: 088-260353
Located nearby the Sabah Tourism office, Diethelm specialises in adventure tourism. They are the white-water rafting specialists, and also offer cycling, as well as the usual range of tours.

WILDLIFE EXPEDITIONS
Room 903, 9th floor,
Wisma Khoo Siak Chew, Sandakan
Tel: 089-219616
Fax: 089-214570 or
331B, 3rd floor, Wisma Sabah
Kota Kinabalu
Tel: 088-254300
Fax: 088-231758
The most experienced operator on Sabah's east coast, with the best guides, taking visitors to Turtle Islands, Sepilok Orangutan Sanctuary, the Lower Kinabatangan River and Gomantong Caves.

FURTHER READING

There are only a few places selling good books and periodicals in Sabah, most of them in Kota Kinabalu. The best range of quality books on Borneo and the rest of Malaysia can be found at Borneo Books, Ground floor, Wisma Merdeka.

Recommended reading

Among Primitive Peoples in Borneo by Evans, Ivor HN. Singapore: Oxford University Press, 1990. A highly readable reprint of a book first published in 1922 on the culture, customs and lifestyles of the people of North Borneo (Sabah).

Culture Shock! Borneo. by Munan, Heidi. Singapore: Times Books International, 1988. Part of a series on different Asian countries, this one dispenses advice on how to behave and understand local customs in Sabah and Sarawak.

Pocket Guide to the Birds of Borneo by Francis, Charles M. Kuala Lumpur: The Sabah Society, 1984. Based on the definitive Borneo bird guide by Bertram E Smythies, this is an ideal companion for the bird lover during a stay in Sabah.

Insight Pocket Guide: Kuala Lumpur, Singapore, 1999. If you are exploring Sabah with the aid of this book, then this guide to the cosmopolitan capital of Malaysia will also go down well. Other books on Peninsular Malaysia in this series include *Insight Pocket Guide: Penang* and *Insight Pocket Guide: Malacca.*

Insight Guide Malaysia. Singapore: Apa Publications, 1999. More than 280 superb photographs and entertaining text capture the heart and soul of this land.

Insight Guide Indonesia. Singapore: Apa Publications, 2001. Packed with information and stunning photographs, the book has detailed information on the whole of this fascinating and beautiful country.

Orang-utan: Malaysia's Mascot by Payne, Junaidi and Andau, Mahedi. Kuala Lumpur: Berita Publishing, 1989. Delightful little book full of information and photographs of these loveable apes, found only in Borneo and Sumatra.

Sabah: The First 100 Years by Leong, Cecilia. Kuala Lumpur Percetakan Nan Yang Muda, 1982. Ignoring the existence of Sabah before the arrival of the British, this looks at the history of the land and its people during the days of the British North Borneo Company through independence and up to 1982.

Wild Malaysia by Cubitt, Gerald and Payne, Junaidi. London: New Holland, 1990. Beautifully written by an expert who has spent more than a decade in Sabah and illustrated with magnificent photographs of the flora and fauna of Malaysia with very good coverage of Sabah.

ACKNOWLEDGMENTS

Photography by

11, 14, 24, 25T, 27, 29B, 30T, 32B, 40, 44B, 47B, 51T/B, 52B, 55, 58T/B, 59T, 61, 62, 66, 68, 73, 74, 76, 77T/B, 78, 79, 80, 81, 83, 84, 90, 94	Tommy Chang
82B	C.L. Chan
8/9	Alain Compost
12, 54B, 92	Alain Evrard
38T	Jill Gocher
10, 11, 13, 16, 21T/B, 22T/B, 23T/B, 25B, 26, 29T, 30B, 36, 37, 38B, 39, 41T, 43, 44T, 45T/B, 52T, 59B, 60, 65B, 67, 85, 86, 87, 88, 89	Wendy Hutton
32T, 33, 41B, 42T/B, 56T/B, 57	A. Lamb
back cover photograph	Philip Little
53, 54T, 65T, 71, 82T	Jock Montgomery
front cover photograph	Navaro/HBL Network
2/3	C. Phillips
35, 47T 48, 49T/B, 50	Albert Teo
Handwriting	V. Barl
Cover Design	Tanvir Virdee
Maps	Berndtson & Berndtson

NOTES

NOTES